Day Trading Strategies

Advanced Techniques to Trade for a Living with Options, Forex, Stocks and Futures.
Tips, Tricks and Tools to Manage Daily Mindset and Psychology for Earn Money Online

By Paul Cohen

Table of Contents

Introduction

Congratulations on purchasing *Day Trading Strategies* and
thank you for doing so.

Trading in the financial markets has caught the eye of several
people across the globe. This has led to an increase in the need
to know how the market works. The most common reason
people have joined trading is to create revenue by making
profits. There are two major forms of trading that are known
as day trading and swing trading. There different ways of
trading, yet they both help an individual to make a profit.

Day trading involves buying financial instruments and later
selling them at a higher price to make profits. On the other
hand, swing trading involves selling financial instruments and
the latter buying them with an aim to make a profit. During
the process of day trading and swing trading, there are several
differences that are sported. These differences include time
spent in each session and the level of risks.

People engaging in day trading usually engage in two forms of
trade. These forms of trade include long trade and short trade.
These two forms of trade are always entered in to by the
situations that preset a trader in the trading process. During
the trading process, there are platforms to help huge funds
with several orders. The most common platform is known as
the high-frequency trading index.

The process of trading encompasses the form of risk management and trading psychology. There are several ways a trader can avoid or minimize risks through the trade process. He or she advised to study market psychology and be calm and accurate when making decisions. There are several people who are in limbo on how to become experts on financial trades. However, there are several simple steps that an individual can use to develop him or herself.

Chapter 1: How Day Trading Works

There are two trading categories of trading in the current global market. They are known as day trading and swing trading. An individual who has an in-depth desire to venture into trading is supposed to know them. However, day trading has been a focal point for several traders. For an individual to understand what it entails, he or she is supposed to know its definition. It can be described as the speculating the securities by specifically selling and buying of financial instruments in the same trading day. During this period, market positions are always closed prior to the market closing for the trading day.

Traders who engage in this type of trade with the aim of getting profits are known as speculators. The methods that are used for day trading are very different from those used in long term trade. Long term trade deals with trade strategies of underlying buying, holding of the financial instruments and investing in value. Day trading is regularly associated with its traders exiting their positions before the market closes. The main aim of this act is to avoid risks that cannot be managed and price gaps that are negative. The negative price gaps can result from the closing one-day prices and opening of the following day prices at the open.

Day trading often involves the use of margin leverage. A good depiction of this phenomenon can be used in the United States of America. Regulation T has the potential to permit initial maximum leverage of up to 2:1. However, many brokers go to levels of promoting up to 4:1 leverage during the moments the leverages are reduced to 2:1 or even less. This is mostly done near the end of the trading day. The market of United States terms traders who trade for more than four days as pattern day traders. These forms of traders have an obligation to maintain a minimum of twenty-five thousand dollars in their accounts as equity.

Traders in the day can end up not fees for interests that are charged for margin benefit. It is because margin interest is a typical charge for the balances that are accrued at midnight. However, this does not brush away the risks of a margin call that are experienced sometimes. A broker is a person who is the determinant of the margin interests because of his or her call. There are several financial instruments that are commonly traded in the modern era day trading. These financial instruments include currencies, stocks, contracts for difference, hosts for future contracts and options. The common future contracts that are traded include interest rates futures, commodity futures, and equity index futures.

There was a time day trading was an exclusive activity. It was a form of trade that was associated with professional speculators and financial firms. A large portion of day trading individuals are the employees of banks and other financial institutions. This group of employees tasked with such roles is always good specialists in managing funds and equity investment. The year 1975 saw the popularization of day trading with several parties joining the trade. It was because the commissions in the United States were deregulated. The rise of electronic platforms for trading was witnessed in the years of 1990s. The volatility of stock prices was also seen during the periods of the dot-com bubble, as represented in figure 1 below. Scalping is a new intraday trading technique that is used by traders in the day trading. It involves holding the trading position for a couple of minutes or seconds.

Figure 1

Profit and Risks of Day Trading

The process of day trading involves sloppy financial leverage and speedy returns are probable. This phenomenon makes the trade to either be extremely profitable or extremely unprofitable. Those people who are described as high-risk profile traders are also greatly impacted by such a phenomenon. These groups of traders have the probability of making enormous percentages of profit or, on the other hand, undergo massive amounts of parentage loss. Day trading trader's individuals are sometimes referred to as bandits or gamblers by other traders or investors. It is because these traders can either make huge amounts of profits or losses during the trade.

There are several factors that can make this form of trade to be very risky while an individual is trading. They include individual trading on trade with low odds instead of trading on a trade that has high odds of winning; the presence of risk capital that is inadequate, which is tied together with overload stress of surviving and presence of poor management of funds which entails poor execution of the trade.

Gains and losses are mostly amplified by the popular usage of buying on margin. The process of buying on margin can be described as the use of borrowed funds. This action usually results in a trader experiencing a substantial loss or gain in a short span during the day. Brokers have the common tendency of allowing bigger trade margins for day traders.

Difference Between Day Trading and Swiss Trading

The main aim of traders in business is to be able to generate profit. There several forms of trading that can be used. For an individual to understand what day trading is about, he or she is supposed to also have insight about swing trading. Having this knowledge and knowing the difference between swing trade and day trade will help them have a clear line of how to perform the trade to impeccable standards.

The first step to understanding swing trading is by getting what its definition is. This is the form of trade that involves a trader to buy or sell financial instruments and hold them for a varied time of a few days. The holding on time of financial instruments can go on to an extended period of several weeks. There are several factors that can make a trader practicing swing trade to be in a sell or buy position. These circumstances are based on technical, quantitative or fundamental valuations by the trader. Such occurrence may mean that a swing trader may take longer working periods than the day trader.

Most people who practice swing trade have a common set of beliefs amongst themselves. They mostly go for the thought of accumulating gains or losses. This process is done in a swift manner that is very slow and smooth compared to day trading. However, there are certain instances where a trader practicing swing trading can experience swings in his or her trades. The results of these swings are always too extreme in two ways. He or she can either gain large percentages of profits or experience huge percentages of loss in a very short time. Individual trading as a swing trader usually does not take part as a full-time trader in the market.

There are four key differences between swing trading and day trading. They include:

- An individual practicing day trading sells or buys financial instruments and liquidates his or her position on the same day. On the other hand, a swing trader upholds his or her position for a variation of days or even weeks.

- A person in day trading is meant to invest a huge number of hours in a day so as to be able to monitor the flow of prices in their portfolios. However, a swing trader is estimated to use few hours in trading as he or she can maintain his or her position for days or weeks.

- Day trading is involved with several sessions of being fast-paced and having adrenaline rushes. It is because there are quick decisions to be made and the trade is fast-paced. This is the exact opposite of people who practice swing trading. It is they are required to be calm when making decisions because they focus more on the long-term return.

- Day trading involves the usage of an advanced system of charting. The charting system is designed to accommodate short intervals of trade. These intervals can be programmed to track one to up to thirty minutes. However, swing traders are prone to using a less complex charting system. These charting systems can be programmed to monitor the market for a varied time of about one to four or five hours.

Short Trades and Long Trades

The terms regarding short trades are common terms to an individual who is participating in stock trading. These terms are majorly used in situations where a trader is either buying or selling first. There are several expectations that a trader always has in mind if he or she is either doing short trade or long trade. When a trader is participating in a short trade, he or she purchases the financial instruments with the aim of selling them at a higher price in the future to make profits. On the other hand, short trade involves a trader selling financial instruments with the intent of later buying them at a lower price so as to make his or her profits.

Long Trade

Various day traders are participants are common in the long trade. They are purchase financial instruments with hopes that they will increase in value. This makes their prices to increase in turn. The term that is mostly used by day traders always buys and long, which are interchangeable. Software developed to help long trade, with buttons that are either marked long or buy. These buttons are used to represent an open position entered by a trader. This position simply means an individual has shares in a certain firm or trade.

When a trader decides to go long, he or she is always interested in purchasing a certain financial instrument. If the decision for such is perused, the potential for profit levels is always unlimited. It is because the prices of the purchased financial instruments can get higher indefinitely. This is despite a day trader participating in small moves. The risks in this form of trade have lower risk potential of the purchased instruments to fall to zero. It is because profits and risks are always controlled by the multiple small moves that are made.

Short Trade

Day traders in short trades always sell their financial instruments before purchasing them. During moments they buy the financial instrument, they hope the prices will have gone down. This the moment they are able to realize their profits because they will be buying the financial instruments at a lower price from that which they had sold. Short trading is one of the most confusing forms of trade because people across the globe are used to buying first before selling. However, one can be able to sell and buy in the financial markets.

There are common terms that are used by traders participating in short trades. These terms include short and sell, which are used interchangeably. Software developed to aid short trade also has buttons marked short or sell. The term short usually means a trader has an open position to shorting some financial instruments. Profit levels are always limited in this situation when compared to the initial amount that was used to purchase the financial instruments. Various traders are used to taking short positions to reduce or minimize risks.

High-Frequency Trading

This is a trading platform that is highly automated used major financial institutions. The large financial institution that is prone to using this trading platform includes investment banks, institutional investors and hedge funds institutions. They use powerful computers because they transact large numbers of commands and orders at high speeds. The high-frequency trading enables traders to make numerous orders and be able to scan several markets. It also gives them the leverage to exchange trade in a couple of seconds. The stated leverages help these institutions to be able to have an advantaged position in the open market.

This system has the ability to use algorithms that are complex to analyze the market. It makes it easy to spot emerging trends in a matter of seconds on a desk. A trader is greatly advantaged when he or she can easily spot the change in the markets. It makes it easy to minimize loss since trades can easily be withdrawn by spreading risks. Several people have been able to realize huge amounts of profits in instances that they correctly predicted the market trends before the system does.

Chapter 2: Trading Platforms and Tools

After learning of day trading and how it works, in this chapter, we begin to look at the trading platforms and tools that help you work better in your day trading techniques. The thing is, when you get into day trading and it is your first time, taking the time to practice and know the know-how is crucial. Practicing means knowing where and what tools you need to go against the professionals that have been doing it for their whole career lives. Jumping in without any idea of what you are doing only means one thing - profits for them.

So, what are some of the tools and platforms and tools that you need with you as you begin day trading?

Brokers

When we look at the term broadly, a broker is someone who buys and sells goods and assets for others. Usually, they are someone more qualified, more experienced in the business than you are. In day trading, a broker is responsible for identifying, negotiating, and sealing deals for you. In day trading, you come across software that takes the place of helping you identify and seal deals like a pro. When you begin day trading, this software is crucial for you. Among the software includes Interactive Brokers, Lightspeed, Trade Station, tasty work and TD Ameritrade.

You may place your trade on these brokers manually from a chart, which we would recommend you do, or you can set up an automated system that would generate orders for you. However, even if you do not want to put in manually data, you should have the ability to monitor price volatility, trading volumes, liquidity, and breaking news. Using this knowledge is key to successful day trading. After all, you aim to make profits on the same day that you put money into the trade.

When you do it, choose a broker that charges per day, not per share, as well as one who provides you with real-time margin and power updates. If you want to trade better from different parts of the world, Interactive Brokers is the best for global exchange and often offers low commissions and high margins.

Market View

A good view of the trading market allows you to understand the risks and gains involved in the trading of your choice and you get to understand better and decide what to buy and sell, concerning three major things;

Liquidity - this is what allows you to get into a stock and exit at a reasonable price.

Volatility - this is the measure of the daily price that traders expected through the day - high volatility means either big profits or significant losses.

Trading Volumes - is the measure of the number of times a stock is bought and sold in a given period, in this case, in the day of trade. When there is a high degree of volume, then it's is an indicator of high interest in the stock, meaning that there is an impending price jump, either up or down.

This trading then means that you need to keep up with the latest stock market news and what events affect changes in the stock. You jot down stocks that you'd like to trade, then learn how they perform in day trading and learn more about your selected companies and the bigger market. Understanding the market view helps you decide on the best order to use to enter or exit a trade. There are two types - market order and a limit order. The market order is usually given at the best price that you find, meaning that there is no price guarantee. Instead, opt for the limit order, which guarantees you of the price, but not the execution. For execution, you should use your judgment, and in day trading, you need to sharpen your judgment. This type of order helps you trade more precisely as it allows you to set your price for buying and selling. In this same strain, when you understand the market view, you will better judge realistically the profits you expect from a trade. You won't have to win all the time to be profitable. According to investopedia.com, many traders win back only 50-60% of their trades. What sets them on the profit path though is that they make more on the wining than on the losing.

Buy and Sell Orders

As we have learned up to this point, trading is more than just buying and selling. As we have touched on this before, market order gives you the market price available, meaning that you get to sell at the price that people are willing to buy from you. This type of trade often works to your advantage when you aim to move into and out of a trade quickly, as in the day trading situation. However, the disadvantage is that, since you do not know exactly what price you will be buying and selling your trade at, if you buy an asset with a tight bid or ask price spread (the difference between the buying and selling price in the stock exchange), you may end up paying the ask price and when you sell, you may pay the bid price.'

The limit order has a sell limit and buys limit. To affect a buy limit order, you will have to wait for the limit price to drop below, while you do the sell order limit at above or within the limit price. Then, there are the stop orders, which are conditional, based on a price that is not yet available when you place the order. The broker then executes them differently. However, once the market price reaches your stop price, it is triggered and becomes a market order.

Indicators on My Charts

When you begin to trade, you notice that many traders spend their time looking for the best moment to enter the markets. When you begin to learn about the trader, you need to get to know some critical indicators that can help you determine the best time to buy or sell. While it is possible to trade by going counter to the trading trend, when you are new to the trading field, going with the trend is the best shot at you making a profit. It is the direction many traders take, and if seasoned traders can take that direction, then you should follow their direction too. You can do this by using trendlines, which helps you identify the direction and strength of a trade so that you know whether you'd be willing to risk it.

According to trade expert Rayner Teo, the obvious interpretation would be that, if the trendline is pointing upwards, it is an uptrend and if it is pointing downwards, it's a downtrend. However, he further advises that, to reason like a pro, you need to understand that the angle of the trend is useful. If the trendline is steep, then the trend is active, while a flatter trendline indicates a weaker trend.

Let's look at the graph below.

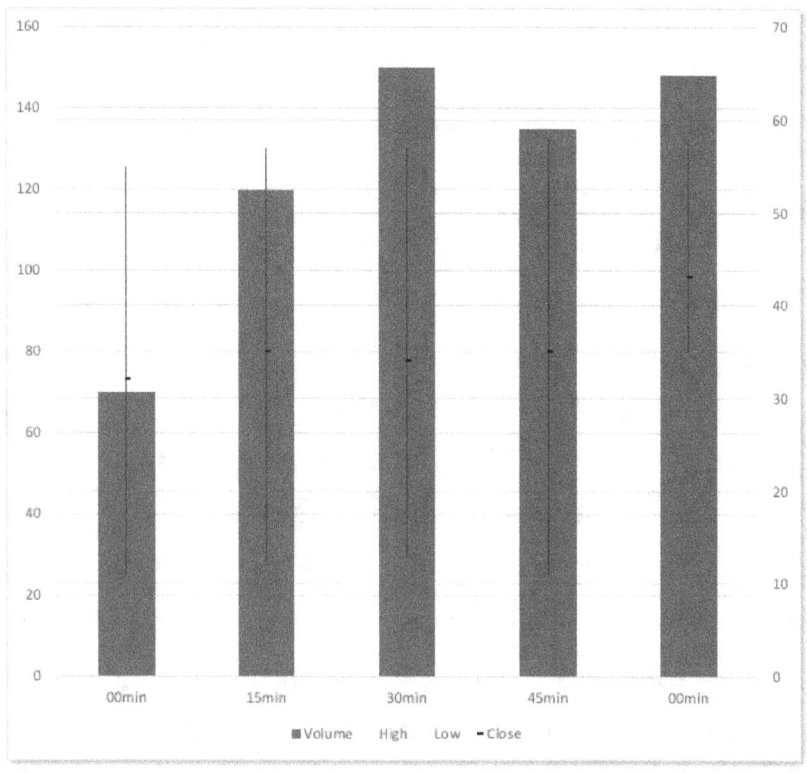

The graph examines how the stock traded for an hour. While there were highs and lows throughout the period, the trend for the hour is generally upward, starting the hour selling 70 volumes at close of 32 and ending the hour at a close of 43 for 148 volumes.

Hotkeys

A hotkey could be one key or a combination of several keys on a computer keyboard that, when pressed, perform a function on the computer more swiftly than if you'd have used a mouse. In trading, hotkeys are essential tools for trade for retail day traders who are not high-frequency traders and have, therefore, taken to using technology to give themselves leverage. Hotkeys are vital commands that you connect with your broker software so that you buy or sell with just the press of the two keys. The most significant advantage of this is that it allows you to navigate fast in the ever-changing, volatile trade market, allowing you to move swiftly to where you may see a potential profit. Most online trading platforms provide you with a combination of keys that would help you perform your tasks on the broker app faster. There are two parts of the hotkey function - the action and then the hotkey. The action is the task that you perform while the hotkey triggers the action.

Hotkeys allow you to make faster executions and orders. While it may not seem like much when you look at it from outside, as it is only a few seconds that it sheds from the regular mouse and click, in the volatile, fast-moving world of trading online, the few seconds become more noticeable, these keys becomes crucial when you have to place multiple orders on a variety of stocks. You get to make cancels faster with hotkeys, especially with the indispensable' Cancel all order function.' The few seconds that the hotkey gives you is what leads to the big difference between you getting a raw deal and dodging a bullet. Let us say you have placed 6 buy-limit orders in 6 different stokes. Then, you begin to see a downward trend from future trades, and they are tumbling down harder than a collapsing tower of paper. That you would need to go through each stock and cancel the order individually, but with the convenience of a 'Cancel all' hotkey, you cancel the orders with just one press of a button.

When you have your broker, it is essential to check with them to find the default order keys linked to the action. According to speedtrader.com, some of the most common hotkeys in day trading are the F1 - F12 keys, but they advise that you first find out that they do not already serve a different function.

Platform Hotkeys

Speed traders defines them as keys used to perform non-trading related actions with regards to the trading software this is important too, though you may probably find perhaps your preference that in the non-trading matter, you prefer to use the standard mouse, point/select and click.

Below are some platform hotkeys.

Refresh keys, which you use to reload a chart or screen.

Zoom in, which allows you to get a closer look at the candle bars

Zoom out, which takes you further out to give you a broader perspective of the chart and follow the trend with a broader perspective.

Switch keys allow you to alternate between different charts or layouts effortlessly.

Real-Time Market Data

This data often gives you the stock volumes traded during the day. Besides giving you the stock prices, through the real-time volume, you can be able to see the other traders in the market who are interested in buying or selling a particular security. Real-time feeds are a vital tool for a beginner as they help in training you in noticing the changes in pricing in real-time. They could also act as a back-up source of data in the event you lose communication with your broker. Several real-time trading charts feed you regularly with data that you need.

Below are a few real-time trading charts.

TradingView - aside from being visually appealing, this site is also a social media site, meaning that you can easily share ideas and charts with other traders. It also allows you to create watchlists (which is covered, more extensively in Chapter 4) and alerts that let you see which stocks look promising.

Yahoo! Finance - it offers IRL quotes from the New York Stock Exchange. It has free interactive charts and gives you an option of more than 100 indicators to select from. However, it also has a premium edition that offers live chat support, fewer ads, as comes with a 28 - day trial.

StockCharts - it offers both free and paid functions, but the free version is limited. Unlike TradingView, though, StockChart is significantly limited as it only allows you a maximum of three indicators, with the free version offering up bland graphs and doesn't allow you to save your screen.

Watchlists and Scammers

Watchlists

A watchlist provides several securities that your broker monitors for potential trading and investing opportunities. To build a useful watchlist, you need to develop many skills sets that give you an edge over most participants. To create a practical watchlist, you are required to understand the modern trading environment, which is crucial as it allows you to create a simple list that you should center on current factors. Then, you get to use the watchlist better to do better research for future items. This understanding also requires you to be going through the list often to get rid of dead stocks so that you only maintain a list of stocks close to buying points. Deductive reasoning is also another skill that you need as it allows you to first create a broad set of criteria for your issues. When you broaden your search, then begin to whittle them down, you get to have a better understanding of the stock market.

Be updated. Because the stock market is fast-changing, you need to continually be in the know so that you can update your watchlist regularly. When you understand the different levels of capitalization, you get to know how catalysts react to different sectors and can make better choices, allowing you to cultivate your investing style, which then makes you comfortable in trading orders.

Scammers

As a beginner, you find yourself targeted by scammers that are in plenty in this mostly
free trading world. Among the many scammers to be aware of are;

Fake Brokers - they may scam you by making moves when the market moves significantly in their favor, or through charging vast amounts of trading commissions and spreads. They may also freeze trading during busy market hours, thus, meaning that you are unable to cancel if the markets begin to go down. Always be on the lookout for brokers who may make withdrawal very difficult, either through charging exorbitant withdrawing fees or asking for excessive identification.

Unregistered Securities - these are often easier to carry out on people new in the trading world. Through a combination of promising higher profits, either by making the differences in spread broader, they may be able to trick you into trading with them.

Community of Traders

Joining a community of traders would be a great way to learn the ropes of the trading world as well as have a database of information that could help you know how to conduct your business. Aside from this, there is also the advantage of being able to identify scammers and how you could avoid them. Below, we look at some of the trading communities that you can join.

Baby Pips

Baby Pips is an excellent forum for beginners. It is an educational forum, operating on an amateur - expert basis. When you join this forum, you put forth a question, and an expert responds to you. It breaks down the basics into easy to learn bits. There are great lessons here, so try it.

Traders Support Club

Ali Crooks, an expert in the field of trading, runs this forum. You pa to join it, but owing to the expertise brimming in the community, many of those that have joined have gone on to become successful traders.

Forex Factory

It is similar to Baby Pips but is more prominent, with a broader pool of experts. This forum is excellent as it ranks contributors according to their impact, thus meaning that you will most likely find your answers as the trolls will often not be ranked high to appear frequently. Here, you find functional analysis and news. Forex Factory was launched in 2004 and currently has 9 sub-forums, ensuring that the experts give you an answer that you find helpful more often.

Trade2Win

This forum is dedicated to the traders and has sub-categories that include beginner, commercial, trading method, traders trading career, and market analysis news. With over 3000 members and over 600 articles, you will most likely find gems in this forum too. In the world of day trading, knowing where to trade and how to go about it is vital. Thus, having a grasp of the tools and platforms is critical.

Chapter 3: Risk and Account Management

Step Risk Management

All organizations face unexpected risks, be it natural calamities or those caused by people. For instance, loss of finances or a member of an organization getting injured. These events can cost your organization to lose a lot of money which may in return, make the company eternally close.

It is therefore important for a company to ensure that one puts strategies that would help in curbing such cases. With risk plan management in your company, you are prepared for a disaster. This is because it will help you to minimize the risk and also the cost you may incur. The risk plan will help you to set aside some amount of money so that it will protect your company in the future if stricken by disaster.

Risk management is a process of finding out the possible risk or disaster before it strikes. These give rooms for the owner of the company to organize his house by setting procedures of avoiding risk and reduce its ineffectiveness. An organization should have a realistic plan of the true level of risk evaluation. A risk management plan should be able to identify and able to deal with the risk. The plans don't need to be costly or should take more time for it to be implemented. Below is a risk management process.

Identifying Risk

You will identify risk by trying to look at it and finding what went wrong. There are many types of risks. They include the environmental risk and authoritarian risk as well as lawful risk and sell and buying risk. If the organization has a risk management tool, it becomes easy. This is because any information will be inserted into the system where it will be available when needed. The information will also be visible to all stakeholders. Being able to identify the risks that may be facing your company gives one a very positive experience.

One can also bring the whole team in the company to take part, which will be of help since they will give useful ideas on ways of managing risks. It will also be able to bring everyone on board and they will give varied experience based on what they have handled. As an employer, you will simply ask everyone to identify the risk they have experienced. The process will promote communication and it will also boost the employee's confidence. They will also be able to learn from each other's experiences. This is because the analysis will be from the management level of the company to the staff members of the company.

Employers can use mind maps that can be used to visualize the possible risk of the plan. They will be useful in inspiring the team members to think outside the box. After that, the management and the group's members will sit down and breakdown the structures to see clearly where risk might emerge. Once you have compiled all the possible issue creates a registered tool that will be used for following and observing all the risk in the plan. When you have all the data it will be easy to manage the upcoming coercion.

Analyzing Risk

What will be the impact of the risk in our organization? Could it make us lose everything we have worked for? Once you have the problem at hand, it becomes very easy to deal with it. In this step, teamwork is also encouraged. Because the team will analyze all the risks and see which one is urgent in dealing with. Prioritizing the risk gives you the idea of how to deal with issues as a whole. You will pinpoint where the team should focus more. They should give workable solutions to each risk. This will speed up the process of dealing with the risk. The determining factors will be time, financial loss and the impact of the risk on the company. If each risk is scrutinized, it will unveil the common topics in the plan and it will simplify the management procedure in the future. When implementing a risk solution is important to map the risk in different credentials, strategies measures, and business progression. It means that the business will have a framework of which it will calculate the risk and make you know the risk they impose.

Controlling and Handling Risk

What can be done to prevent the risk from taking place? If we are already in that mess, how are we going to salvage it? The moment the risk has been identified, it becomes easy to administer medication. You will table your medication plan and dispatch it. You will start with the risk with the highest priority. Assign duties to the team members so that they can help you in dealing with the problem. For mitigation to be effective, you will need help from the team resources. With time you will be having a database of the past plans. It will be easy to deal with others' risks because you will have the risk logs with you. You will not be practical rather than reacting to the advance for more treatment. There are four major groupings.

Transferring a risk means that the whole or part of the risk can be moved to a certain part, but some cost will be incurred. Avoiding a risk means that no activity will be carried out that will have risk. This may be the best way to deal with risks; for instance, not joining a business because you want to avoid losing an also it makes you avoid the possibility of making a profit. Regarding retaining a risk, there are two methods of retention: the self-insurance and captive insurance. Retention risk means the losses from the company or organization will be retained due to the decision from the business company. Controlling risk can be done by either avoiding the risks or by controlling the loss from the organization.

For risk management to be effective, it should ensure that all members of the organization are committed. All the policies and methods should be established. The staff should have clear roles and responsibilities and are very accountable. The teams should also have adequate resources and tools to be able to deal with the risk. If this is done, the benefits could be there will be saving of funds, point in time profits possessions populace and property. Having a safe and conducive environment for the workers, visitors, and also customers. There can be also a reduction in the legal liability and make an increase in the stability of the operations.

Trading Psychology

Trading psychology is referred to as a trader's mental state as well as their emotions which enable them to make sound decisions which in return will dictate their success as well as failure in the trading business. It represents the character and behavior of individuals which affects their actions when trading. For a businessman to succeed in the trading business, they need to ensure that they are good when it comes to trading psychology. This is because trading psychology is helpful in ensuring that a trader makes informed decisions for his company. Their mental, as well as emotional aspects, are helpful in ensuring that they make the right decisions.

Greed and fear, as well as regrets, are emotions that play a vital role in the trading business. In a trading business, greed can be important as well as destructive. This is because when one is greedy, they will always be driven by the desire to make more and more money. A trader should, therefore, utilize it in a good way in order to ensure that they benefit from it. They should learn the situations where they should use greed and when they should not.

Greed is described as an irresistible feeling which makes one want to be in possession of more things than they actually need. Greed is something that is very difficult to overcome. It requires one to have a lot of discipline in order for them to overcome it. Greed makes a trader want to make more money than they already have. Greed is said to have great results when utilized in the bull market. This is because the more a trader stays in the trading business, the more he or she gains experience. The experience enables them to be able to explore all the available opportunities, which helps them to create more wealth. Greed is only destructive when one invests, and then the stock market drops. They may find themselves making losses which are not so good for business.

A trader can, however, overcome greed by ensuring that they come up with a trading plan. The plan will normally be centered on balanced investment decisions. This will help a lot in ensuring that one is not guided by emotions when making business decisions. A trader can even set rules which they cannot go against when it comes to trading. They can also set a specific amount of money that they are ready to win and even to lose daily. They will only have that amount so once they exhaust it, they will just stop and wait to trade another day. This will help them in ensuring that they are disciplined when it comes to investing since they will invest an amount of money that they are ready to lose.

Fear is defined as something that one perceives as a threat to their income and also to their profits. Fear is also beneficial because it encourages the trader to hold back whenever they want to take any step in the trading process. It can also be destructive as well as useful, which will depend on when it is applied. A trader may feel the urge to invest in something, but because of fear of failing, they will stop. For example, whenever a trader receives any bad news about the stock market or even about the market in general, they tend to panic since they do not know whether they are going to make losses or not.

There are those whose fear may lead them to liquidate their shares in the market while there are those who will just continue investing. By withholding their shares, it may save them when the prices in the stock market fail but they may lose opportunities to make more money because of the same fear. It is therefore important for a trader to ensure that they find ways of overcoming their fears, especially in situations that they feel like they could make losses. They should take calculated risks in order for them to ensure that they do not make losses after investing their shares in the market. The traders can also study the market which will help them to be able to identify areas that they can invest in without fear.

The last emotion to take into consideration when trading is regret. Many businessmen have found themselves engaging themselves in the trading process because of regrets in the other businesses they have engaged in. If not careful, they may find themselves regretting investing in the trade business in a hurry. The regrets will come in when they lose money after investing. It is therefore important to ensure that as a trader, you carry out thorough research before investing your money in any business. It is important to ensure that you are of sound mind when engaging in the trading business in order for you to be able to become successful in it.

Traders are encouraged to ensure that they carry out research in the areas that interest them. They can attend seminars where they will be educated on all the trading areas. This will be of great help in ensuring that one overcomes is fear and also take risks without making losses. A trader can also asses his or her performance every often. They can also review their returns which will give them the go-ahead in investing when other opportunities present themselves. They will also be able to tell whether they are making profits or losses hence the need for assessment every so often.

Chapter 4: Building your Trading Watch List

A Trading Watch List

As an active day trader, you must create a trading watch list. Basically, this is a list where you record the daily share prices of a group of stocks over time. It acts like a menu for the trading day. Based on the fundamental and technical new catalyst, a trading watch list should have active stocks that are ready to trade. It can either be done on the notepad, a spreadsheet, or even on paper. There are many software programs and other utilities that help in generating a watch list. It can also be provided by some brokerage houses where you pay a minimal charge, or for free.

A trader can have more than one watch list, but there are two specific watch lists that every active trader should never mess; a general watch list and a dynamic watch list. The general one may be composed of hundreds of stocks that are familiar to the trader. Every trader should also narrow down from the general watch list and come up with an active stock watch list every trading day before the market opening. This watch list should have stocks that the trader has been watching for days or weeks, that may be about to set up for a technical movement. Unlike the general list, the active trade list should not contain too many stocks. It should have a handful of ripe stocks that the trader is comfortable to trade. In other words, a general watch list may contain shares that the trader has already purchased recently or in the past, while the active watch list should contain stocks that the trader is considering to purchase. For example, let's say that you are an active trader with ten positions on average at any given time. Usually, you will be tracking several stocks, so that you can purchase another position from the watch list immediately after one position has been sold. This will help you avoid a situation where at any given time, you have a lot of idle cash in your trading account.

A watch list is convenient for many different reasons. For example, let's say that you have done your research and found a company that you feel is sound and has a promising potential, but the stock value seems to be currently high or overvalued. You decide to wait for a better convenient time so that you can buy. You will use the watch list to track the stock price and generate charts to monitor the stock trends. That way, you will be able to know the best time to purchase that stock.

Building Your Trading Watch List

Stocks in Play

When a stock is widely believed to be a takeover target, it is said to be in play. Day traders widely trade stocks in play because their volatility produces reasonable risks and trading opportunities. When company stocks have less volatility, they move slowly, and they only have a reasonable price change only when the company shows good or bad trading outcomes. This may occur only a few times in a year. Such companies are ideal for investors looking for returns in the long-term. Long term investors buy shares in these companies, which have good prospects, with shares moving slowly in the right direction, and it matters less to them if the share price doesn't move much intraday. But day traders buy and sell stocks during stock market opening hours and exit the trade before the day ends. Sometimes they even trade for a few minutes or an hour and exit the market. They, therefore, require more action than investors. They need stocks that move and produce price swings so that their trade becomes worthwhile. Such fluctuations in prices leave enough room for them to realize profits, after paying the association fees charged by stockbrokers for buying and selling shares.

Stocks in play also have a large volume. Day traders are after quick entries and exits, and they want liquid stocks. That means they can buy and sell shares in the stock on demand. A stock that doesn't have good liquidity and my cost the broker time to strike a promising buying or selling deal. The broker is unable to negotiate the deal that the trader wants to buy or sell at. For day traders, this is a problem because it means the difference between a profitable trade and a non-profitable one. Day traders are guided by trade volumes of shares that are traded each day to arrive at what they consider good liquidity for them. For most traders, one hundred thousand shares traded per day would be their minimum, while some other traders may require a million shares.

Stocks in play will change in one day. An ordinary stock will be put in play by the company news which is typically released early in the morning, and it will vary depending on the nature of the new, whether it is good or bad. Sometimes good news for traders may be bad news for investors. Some of the big companies like Apple, Amazon, and Facebook have stocks that are always in play, and day traders will have these stocks constantly in their watch list. This is because they have large volumes of trades and traded shares. This is where a day trader looks for excellent trading opportunities, and proper levels to trade from.

Nowadays, most of the broker platforms include a section where they list trending shares. This section lists a number of shares that have trended in the day, or that are currently trending. Other websites have free stock screening tools that help traders to find stocks that are in rapid movement, intraday and break out pre-market. These are websites like Marketwatch and Busystock. Breakout shares and top lists for trending UK shares are produced by ADVFN. They also have apps like Seeking Alpha, with live news feeds that are accessible for you. Big company news and breaking news are quickly reported by news channels like CNN, BBC, Reuters, and Bloomberg. Up to the minute, relevant news for day traders is also provided by channels like Stocktwits.

Float and Market Cap

As an active day trader, it is crucial to understand the link between company size, risk, and return potential. Such information is vital as you lay the foundation to pursue long-term trading goals. With such knowledge, you can build a balanced watch list that comprises different market caps.

Market cap means market capitalization. It expresses the stock value of all the company shares. To arrive at the market cap of an entity, multiply the entities' shares by the stock price. An Entity with $50 million in shares with each share trading at $20 then $10 billion will be its market cap. Market cap is necessary because it helps traders to understand and compare the size of different companies. Market cap helps you to know the worth of different companies in the open market. It also helps you to understand how the market perceives a particular company and mirrors what investors and traders are ready to pay for its stock.

Large-cap stocks: $10 billion and over is their stock market value. Typically, these are reputable companies that produce quality goods and services. They experience steady growth and have a history of consistency in dividend payments to their shareholders. Their brand names are familiar to national and even international consumer audience. They are dominant players in their respective industries of the establishment.

They are ideal for conservative investors since they pose less risk as they have less growth potential.

Mid-cap stocks: Typically, these are businesses with a minimum market value of $2billion and a maximum market value of 10$billion. In other words, their market value is between $2billion and $10 billion. They are medium-sized, established companies with growth potential. Such companies are either experiencing rapid growth, or there is an expectation that they will grow rapidly in the near future. They are in the stage of boosting their competitive advantage and widening their share of the market. This is a crucial stage since it determines their ability to attain maximum potential. In terms of risk, they have less risk in comparison with new startups. When it comes to potential, they offer more potential than blue-chip companies since they are expected to continue to grow until they reach full potential.

Small caps: their market stock value ranges from $300 million to $2 billion. They are growing businesses that are just emerging in the industry. They are the riskiest and the most aggressive and rely on niche marketing to survive in the industry. Due to limited resources, they are vulnerable to economic shocks. They are susceptible to intense competition and market uncertainties. Since they are new startups, they have high growth potential in the long-term, and they are ideal for investors who can cope up with volatile stock price swings in the short-run.

Float, on the other hand, is the number of shares, which are available for trading by the general public. Unlike the market cap that calculates the total stock value of all company shares, free-float does not include locked-in shares. Locked-in shares are those that are held by company employees and the government. Market cap can be affected by several factors. When there is a significant change in the value of shares, either up or down, this can have an impact on the market cap. Market cap can also be impacted when the number of issued shares changes. Market cap can be diluted when warrants are exercised on the stock of the company because the number of shares outstanding will increase. This is because such an exercise is often carried out below the shares market price, hence has the potential to impact on the market cap. On the other hand, issuing a dividend or a stock split typically doesn't alter the market cap.

To build a stable watch list, comprising large-cap, mid-cap, and small-cap stocks, a trader will have to evaluate their time horizon, risk tolerance, and financial goals. A balanced watch list comprising all the market caps may be ideal in helping to reduce the investment risk.

Pre-Market Gappers

Pre-market trading refers to trading activities that take place between 8 am and 9:30 am EST every trading day. This is usually before the regular market session begins. Traders and investors monitor the pre-market trading period to judge the direction and the strength of the market while waiting for the regular trading session. During the pre-market activity, there is limited liquidity and volume. Wide bid-ask spreads is a common thing during the pre-market period. The type of orders that can be used during this period is limited by many retail brokers, even though they offer pre-market trading. As early as 4 am, direct-access brokers begin to allow access to the pre-market activity to start. It is crucial to bear in mind that there is limited activity during this pre-market period.

The most reliable types of stocks that are beneficial to trade during pre-market activities are gapper or dumper. They are usually viable during the seasons when earnings for various companies are reported. During such season, these stocks gap with the volume either up or down. They are usually triggered by a primary catalyst such as press releases, news, or earnings reports. They can also be reacting to rumors or analyst upgrades or downgrades. It is important to note that stocks tend to get more 'tradability,' follow-through, and consistent volume when they are gapped in reaction to earnings reports and guidance. As you trade during pre-market activity, you should always know that this period is characterized by fewer participants, wider spread, and thin liquidity. It is not advisable to trade pre-market unless there is a substantial volume gap that is being driven by a catalyst. Waiting for the market to open is the most suitable option for most traders.

Real-Time Intraday Scans

A stock scanner is a screening tool that uses user-selected criteria and trading metrics to search the market and find stocks that meet the set standards. They can be modified to find the most suitable candidates that match user-specific filters using technology. They have helped to streamline the time-consuming task of attempting to trace new trading opportunities. This makes it efficient and convenient for traders to quickly find potential stocks. It is an essential tool for traders and investors due to its speed and convenience.

Real-time intraday scans are essential for day traders, and they work to spot stocks during market hours. They produce results that are highly sensitive to time and require the trader to analyze them quickly on the fly to determine whether a trade should be made. Intraday patterns require quick action as they develop and fade within a short period. Real-time intraday scans help day traders to maximize the limited time duration they have to make decisions before the patterns shift. They are a great way to introduce a trader to new stocks, especially when they search the whole market for candidates. These new stocks can then be added to the watch list. These new stocks can then be monitored to get acclimated to the liquidity, trade volume, spread, and the pace of the price action. A trader can dramatically narrow his field by modifying the filters to search only for stocks that meet his desired price range and minimum volume requirements.

The ability of the scan to produce accurate results will be determined by the tightness of your parameters. It is good to make sure that the parameters have been set correctly, to provide precise intraday alerts. Always make sure to validate the accuracy of the scan results, whether you are scanning for pattern ups or pre-set ones. By prudently leaning the necessary programming, you can customize your scan to produce the results you need. Always remember that scans are not intuitive, and they may miss the context that determines how effective the pattern is.

Planning Trade Based on Scanners

When correctly used, scanners are helpful, enabling the trader to wave through the market noise and concentrate on the most qualified stocks. But as a trader, it is always important to keep in mind that the results produced by a scanner only act as filters. You still need to carry out careful analysis to determine their credibility. Make the necessary confirmation of the set-ups before you consider a trade. The reliability and accuracy of scanners can be doubtful, especially if such results have been produced by pattern-based scanners. Sometimes you can spread your trade too thin between candidates when you use scanners in the wrong way. This may create opportunities for you to lose money faster than you expect

Make sure that you understand the criteria better and test the screened results to gauge how reliable the scanner is. Therefore, do not jump head over heels to pop up stocks in a scan. Familiarize yourself with the stock by applying your triggers the moment the candidates become validated. Therefore, you should take the time to analyze the screened results thoroughly and plan your trade well based on those stocks.

Chapter 5: Support and Resistance Levels

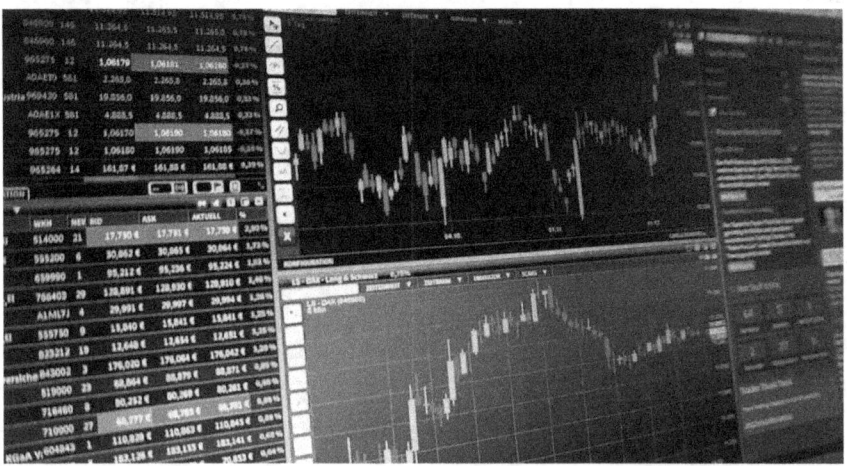

In order to understand the meaning of support and resistance levels, one needs a clear background check on what day trading entails. As discussed in the other chapter, day trading is the process of having a forecast in securities. This involves the purchase and sale of financial instruments within the same day of trading. The closure of business here is dependent on the end of the business day. Trading in this kind of manner is based on speculation. The probability of profit and loss is not defined. Owing to this, you may experience losses and profit in any instance.

For one to engage in this type of trade and survive, one needs a well-structured strategy that will ensure you are speculating the right way. In a nutshell, day trading can be referred to as the acquisition or disposal of securities within a single trading day. The background of day traders is one that is full of funding and well-conversant with the business field. Their game is fixed on short-term strategies that have a high value of leverage. In this sense, they tend to capitalize on shifts in prices no matter how remote it may seem.

Day traders thrive on events that cause shifts in price. This is usually in the short term. The news is their biggest asset. Trading in the news will ensure that they have information concerning market psychology. This includes the announcement on various interest rates, statistics, market expectations, and corporate earnings. Day traders employ numerous strategies in their day to day activities. These strategies include but are not limited to High-frequency trading, range trading, scalping and news-based trading. The idea of day trading is fixed behind the misconception of getting rich quickly. Thus, within a short period of time. This is often what attracts people to engage in this kind of trading. People who engage in this kind of trading without sufficient knowledge often end up in losses. Despite the risky nature in the manner of speculation that characterizes day trade, it is a lucrative business that puts food on the table for many lads. Its risky nature is what makes it so lucrative.

Behind every success story, there is a significant struggle story. People who engage in day trading have a view of making a profit. However, this is not always the case as some people result in irreparable loss. Before engaging in this particular type of trade, one needs an inner understanding of the factors at hand. The probability of making a profit is often lower.

Support and Resistance Levels

In the business world, especially in forex and stock markets, support and resistance levels act as yardsticks towards the determination of a price and are characterized by numerous f security. The price is usually set at a point in which it is thought to stop and start reversing. The support and resistance levels are dynamic in nature and are characterized by numerous speculations in the price without necessarily settling on the right price. Technical analysts employ this method in a bid to determine the price. This type of method has grown a lot of fame in the recent past. Support and resistance are diverse in a manner that they showcase themselves in different ways. These words can be used to refer to barriers in the chart. Those factors that act in the opposite direction of pushing a price towards a certain direction.

Support refers to a level of price whereby there is demand for a specific type of securities. This concentration of demand has an alternative effect of preventing the downfall of the price level. Asset or securities and shares are directly related. This means that when the price of assets and securities falls, the demand for shares escalates. When demand for hares increases, a support line is thus formed. The effect on the resistance zones will be to rise because of the sell-off when prices escalate. The identity of a zone of support or resistance creates potential points of entry or exit from the market. Owing to the fact that when a price reaches support or resistance points, it will react in different ways. It may separate itself from the support and resistance levels, or it may cause havoc to the price level and proceed in its direction to the point that it meets with the next support and resistance factors.

Trading under these factors of support and resistance is premised on the belief that these factors would not be broken. Dependent on whether the price is affected by the support or resistance levels or events desire to breakthrough, day traders are always keen to place their bets on the direction that the price will take. Upon determination of whether the choice is correct, there are a number of things that happen. If the price favors the trader, the direction is very advantageous to the trader. If any situations go haywire, the position can come to an end with a small loss being felt.

Traders with experience in this field are often keen to make observances as in the field of day trade. For instance, how a certain underlying asset is prevented from moving in a certain direction owing to the fact that price levels are curtailing this movement. For instance, trader A had stock in hold between January and June. His anticipation was that the value of the share would escalate. Trader A realizes that the price fails to favor him completely that business month and, in fact, they stay stagnated. Trader A, upon noticing this fact, will then decide to fix the price at a resistance level. This resistance level is to act as a ceiling to the market price. When the ceiling is done, the market prices are prevented from sky-rocketing. This is a practice that will be of much aid to trader A in disposing of his or her shares.

Support price level forms the direct opposite of resistance price levels. They have an effect of acting as a floor. This floor acts in a preventive manner. It prevents the price levels from dropping way below. From the basic knowledge of a floor, a floor is what rests below everything in a household. The support levels ensure that a trader does not incur a severe loss. When identifying the level of support, one may be mistaken to be attracted to a good buying opportunity. These two phenomena go hand in hand. You will always be obliged to purchase when the prices are in downfall, and so when including a support level, it has to be that the price is in a downfall. This is also the point at which price levels are pushed upwards in the market. This is because they have reached a point that they cannot drop anymore and the only direction it can take is to move upwards.

Support and resistance, however, have diverse meanings to the extent that one should not rely on the contextual meaning alone. For instance, when the price levels of an asset are constant and are prevented from moving upwards or downwards. This is known as a static barrier and it has grown fame when it comes to supporting and resistance curves. Financial assets tend to escalate or drop over a given period of time. A common practice is that barriers to a particular price level will always fluctuate over time. For instance, when the market is on an upside trend, resistance levels will be formed when the market disintegrates and the price levels are no longer in an upward move but now stagnating and falling back. These factors are often as a result of not re-investing your profits and focusing on short-term uncertainties. These are factors that you have no foresight on, yet you prefer to indulge in. The consequences of these actions will be that the price goes into a plateau or stagnated level.

The focus of numerous day traders is often on the price of an asset as it drops towards the support line. History has it that this level of support has often acted in the opposite direction with regards to dropping the price of an asset. With this in mind, a trader would be inclined to acquire such kind of assets due to the mere fact that there exists a support line. This support line acts in the advantage of day traders since the only direction a price takes after hitting a support line is upwards.

The market may also be on a falling spree. This refers to the price levels of various assets falling down significantly. Those that were at their peaks will experience a significant drop. This kind of drops is what trader's eye for. Owing to the fact that this is a zone whereby the price levels have always dropped even with reference to the past, traders enter into such deals with a short-term goal of ultimately selling off the assets. The pressure is often felt that, in turn, forces the individual to engage in a sell-off before the prices fall further.

The strength of support or resistance of a particular identified level is dependent on the fact that how many times in the past that the price has been able to depart from it. The identified levels of resistance and support often create entry or exit points to the market. This is as a result of the fact that this zone has prices that have been most influential to an asset direction. At this level, traders have an attitude that there is an underlying value in the assets that they possess. This, in turn, makes disposal or acquisition of the said assets difficult. When this happens, prices do not go high or drop because there is no trading.

Finding Support and Resistance Levels

From the above section, we have already gathered what support and resistance means. We have had an in-depth understanding of the various factors that lead to the dropping of price levels to the support line and escalation to the resistance level. Price levels tend to operate within these constraints until they reach a breaking point and move away from the market. There are various methods that a trader can employ in a bid to secure support and resistance. They include but are not limited to Gann lines, trend lines, chart patterns, Fibonacci lines, and pivot points.

PBV Charts

These charts refer to a standard procedure of volume histogram re-aligned against the forces of price. These charts have an effect on determining the level of purchasing or selling interest at a given price level. These charts can be formulated in a number of charting applications. They are relatively simple in nature and are easy to use. The chart involves three major elements that include: the volume strength that provides for the number of shares being traded at a given price. This is often denoted by the horizontal length of the histogram. The volume type has an effect of tabulating the amount of shares purchases vis-a-vis the ones sold. There is a test known as the Successful Reaction Test which indicates the various times that a stock has been able to bounce off its support line. The three factors working in unison have an effect of determining the merits of various price levels.

Gann Lines

The Gann lines adopt a school of thought that the stock market is cyclic in nature. This is owing to the fact that it is characterized by the same movements over and over. Gann lines are a system of technical analysis that comprises a Gann fan, which is made of various lines known as Gann angles. The angles are then implemented over the price of assets in order to show instances of support and resistance. The resulting image plays a big role in aiding analysts' forecast on the changes in price. Gann fans have no absolute formula. They, however, require a background in the comprehension of degrees of slop.

Pivot Points

This is a technique that was developed by floor traders, especially in the market for commodities. Its effect was to predict potential points where the prices bounce back. These points are crucial in that they are the ones that tend to set the basis for entry or exit from the market. These pivot points are calculated in forex in order to determine when the factor surrounding a market will change from severe to bearable. The pivot points often denote the points at which support and resistance appeared. Pivot points are known to work best when the business capital is in liquidation. Pivot points can be points of correspondence to trend lines and Fibonacci lines. Pivot points refer to discrepancy when it comes to levels of price. The basic formula of employing highs and lows together with the previous closes has been a popular means.

Trend Lines

A trend line that indicates the general course of a phenomenon. This is a geographical feature that sets points throughout the graph. This, in turn, helps in the determination of various factors since there is an evident line that helps in the back-tracking of events. In the financial world, a trend line is one that is able to co-relate the way a price moves in correspondence to security. The trend line uses pivot points in that a diagonal line is drawn connecting three or two pivot points. A support trend line is a line that forms when the price of securities falls and settles at a pivot point. When security prices increase and settle at a point of pivot, then a resistance trend line is formed.

Chapter 6: Price Action, Candlesticks and Trade Management

Price Action and Mass Psychology

Price Action

Price Action in trading is an activity whereby a trader makes decisions according to the price in the market. Price action is determined by the market and often determined by the price of the commodity.

A customer behavior drives the price of a commodity and often the price action trader is not involved in the things that happen in the market but rather is interested only in the price. For instance, a price action trader will buy a commodity at a cheaper price anticipating to rise in the future and make profits. This, however, is not the case every time as some markets are unpredictable. Price Action trading, however, can be a good fortune if the future markets are predictable and is good for non-perishable goods since it can stay for long in stores as they await to be sold. The price action is always determined by mass or crowd psychology. This is the willingness to buy or sell at a given period, mainly to suit their situation. In forex trading, price action traders also follow trends according to the crowd mentality to buy or sell and if one masters the art of the market, then they are sure to make profits.

Mass Psychology

This can also be referred to as a 'crowd on herd' mentality. This is likened to a herd of cows where they do almost everything at the same time. The unison like minds is called a herd mentality where they think alike according to their situation. In forex trading, buyers and sellers can determine a market through their thinking and this affects the price. Price Action traders always depend on the crowd mentality to make their decisions. Mass thinking also helps in making future decisions for the markets. If you can predict the future market, you can be sure of earning heavy profits when the prices go high. Mass psychology in price action trading also helps in the flow of currency due to a busy trading environment, unlike in off-peak season when the buyers and sellers or demand and supply are not an equilibrium.

Price Action and Mass psychology work together in a collective manner such that when the popular trend is on, the price action traders strike too. The behavior of buyers can think along due to the economic situation or the cost of living in certain regions. This can affect the forex trading patterns, and one wrong move in this can accrue to losses. Many business-minded people thing trading on price is lucrative, but the reality of the matter is that nothing is easy when the future market is unknown and when dealing with unpredictable markets. However, all is not a walk in the park for mass psychology and it has some disadvantages that can affect the forex business Mass psychology has its disadvantages and risks when followed in forex trading.

Fear

This is among the big distraction in the forex business. Traders tend to move with the crowd and trade in fear of making losses. When a crowd decides to take a turn in one direction, some will want not to be Left behind in the trading pattern created by others instead of sticking to the plan. This is hazardous as you may not know the strategies of other forex traders. This form of anxiety can be controlled by training the mind to think in a particular way and not be dismayed by popular opinion. Always remember not every popular say is right for your way of doing things might be even better. This can also be clustered as greed as some people want to have more than they can even chew. Always have in mind that business should give proper and realistic profits and trying to pop in of loopholes in business can be a trap, and unrealistic patterns can occur to losses.

In this form, one can act out of fear because of the following.

Doubt

Acting out of doubt is very dangerous for any business, and one should be clear on what they want to achieve with their trading pattern. Most traders move with the crowd when they are not sure, and you might find yourself following them when they are all wrong. This can, however, be avoided by having the right decision and understanding the business before joining it.

Loss

This is every businesses' worst nightmare, and everyone joins the business to make profits. However, in between, there is learning and failure that might frustrate a trader. Fear can come in when you are afraid of incurring losses, and you might end up making bad decisions. When trading on mass behavior, one can fear missing out on the trend and ends up making hurried decisions.

Greed

This is a vice in every adventure and having self-control in business is a remedy. Some forex traders are greedy and want to benefit in every pattern even when there is a plan is not supporting the trend. The fear of being left out in huge junk of money can lead many price action traders to make unnecessary decisions that might hurt the business to its core.

False Security

This is a self-distraction that comes in when the mass is moving in a certain direction, and it gives you the benefit of the doubt that they are right even when you know it is not. Some traders depend on mass behavior to make their decisions, and that is so wrong. You cannot follow the masses blindly because you think they might be right and you on the wrong side. Use your instincts to judge a situation when you are not sure. False security is hazardous in that not everything the masses do turns out to be true or correct and should be avoided like the plague.

Not Sticking to the Plan

This is an important rule that forex traders should stick to create a good report and straight trading pattern. As it has been playing along in the movies and popular sitcoms, many incidences where the actors do not stick to the plan, things always fall apart, this is no difference to forex trading and other forms of businesses. Following the masses can mislead at times as compared to sticking to a certified plan. Some are known for staking high in mass behavior and is not recommended at all. What if the trend was a lie and you had put millions in it? Will you lose all of it? Sticking to the plan is simply not being greedy and controlling oneself or not emotionally trading but trading on tested patterns and plans.

Bullish and Bearish Candlesticks

Bullish candlestick is a pattern that is used to determine the future of forex trading by how the market behaves during a particular day. From the word bull, which means huge, a price action trader predicts a price rise the following day, thus the bullish candlestick. Just from the word candle is candlestick derived where the pattern takes a form of a source of light and is arranged in a manner that shows changes in the sizes depending on the anticipated forex market. The bullish candlestick pattern can also be termed as a two-candle pattern that shows or predicts a massive shift. This can be shown on a diagram where a bearish candle (which in this case is small) is followed by a bullish candle (which is big). The bullish candlestick pattern in a chart form is characterized by a small back body before a white big body which is considered huge or bulls.

Here are some of the characteristics that can help in determining a bullish candlesticks pattern for perfect forex trading.

How to Recognize

Downtrend- when there is a prevailing deterioration of the forex market, that means a bullish pattern is predetermined by price action traders, which make them predict the mass behavior of buyers. This can be a prevailing trend for a couple of days in forex trading.

The black body appears- when a bearing candlestick is seen (which is the white body) appears on the first day, it means the forex market or prices are expected to go higher any minute.

White body covers black body- when the bullish covers the downtrend, it means that the business is looking fine, and the prices might shoot up any moment and forex traders are expected to do big business and win at the close of the day.

Pattern Requirements

Flexibility

As stated earlier, the white body covers a larger part of the candlesticks as compared to the black body which should not belong and should be engulfed by the white one.

Mass Behavior

The behavior of a trader in a bullish pattern is seen where the market starts on a downtrend on the first day and this is characterized by a black body which disappears on the second day and the prevailing low market is derailed and surplus buying supersedes selling which in turn increase profits mostly for forex traders trading on price action.

On the other side, the bearish candlestick is the opposite of the bullish pattern, where the former is characterized by the black candlestick to determine the behavior of the market. According to the previous explanation, a forex trader can do trading at the close of business. This can favor a trader in that if there is an increase in a trend where it follows a large downtrend, a trader who trades in price action can find it easier to sell as compared to other times.

Candlesticks Patterns

From the examples given above is bullish and bearish candlesticks patterns; a candlestick is a behavior of prices demonstrated through graphs popularly known as a candlestick chart that traders use to predict market change. The patterns are arrived at through predicting criteria depending on the current market. Just from the word candle, the graph is designed in a way that the white and black candlesticks take the shape of a candle to represent the highs, lows, and movement of the market in a financial period. These are some of the common candlestick patterns that forex traders use to determine or rather predict the market they anticipate in minting profits from.

Three White Cops

Like the word itself, white cops are the three long candlesticks that have higher closes, respectively. This means that the bearish candlesticks are near the highs, which are considered as the peak market and the lows considered as reversal signals. The bottom one is a red light that the market is not good and predicts losses.

Black Body

This is a situation where the body is black and medium-sized and represents a high opening price as compared to closing price. When the opening is high, it is considered a bullish and at the closing price, the downtrend occurs and leaves a bearish signal.

Big Black Candle

Just like the black candle, this has highs and lows but is a bit longer compared to the former. The opening prices are high, and the closing prices are expected to be low, thus registered as the bearish pattern.

Big White Candle

This is the direct opposite of the big black candle. The white candle is presumably long and has opening prices of lows and closing of high because of its bearish nature. Therefore, this means that a forex trader will predict a good chance in the market on day 2 as it gives a bullish signal.

Morning Star

From the word morning, it means that the star is already down because the sun is up, and this translates to the behavior of the candle. In this case, the black candle will appear then followed by a tiny white candle on the bottom and then closed by a second white body.

Evening Star

As the name suggests, during the evening, stars start showing when the sun sets, and it is always a peak time for it is their turn to shine bright. Same to the candlesticks, the evening star will have a big white candle at the beginning and a small star at the top followed by a black one on the second day. The top place of the star shows the highs and represents a signal of the bullish pattern.

Shooting Star

This is a star that has a head and a long tail. Unlike the long upper shadow, the head which forms the star is at the bottom and makes an uptrend.

Long Upper Shadow

This candlestick has its head slightly above the bottom. The star can be either black or white and often called a bearish signal in some sections along with price levels.

Trade Management Based on Price Action

Price Action in trading is an activity whereby a trader makes decisions according to the price in the market. Price action is determined by the market and often determined by the price of the commodity. A customer behavior drives the price of a commodity and often the price action trader is not involved in the things that happen in the market but rather is interested only in the price. This means that traders who trade depending on the price action make their decisions based on price movements, unlike other forms of business which use set indicators.

Trade management is where trade is controlled after executing it to serve the purpose of creating profits in any way possible as well as avoiding risks that are prone to businesses. Not every trader, however, is gifted with managerial skills that help govern online trading to enable them to maximize profits. For any forex and any business to work, there must be trade management, which takes almost a bigger percentage of the work done to bring profits home and this does not happen when the strategies are not followed to the latter.

After having a price action trading format, it is also important to outline the steps that can be taken to minimize the chances of losses at the close of business.

Price Action Trading Steps

As it has been discussed above in the patterns followed to make profits through price action patterns, the end game is to have many chances of winning as possible and probably wins at the end of the day. Also, mastering entry and exit levels in price action trading is paramount is it help in double chances unlike only putting everything on one outcome. The two stated steps are scenario and opportunities which can be seen according to your strengths.

Scenario: before you trade on price action, make sure you outline the form of environment you are in at the time of trading t make sure you hit the right market with the right approach. This can be through identifying the bullish and bearish form of trading that suits your plan.

Opportunities: price action trading may also have different chances on the same scenario and a trader can pick what best suits their instincts. The opportunity is like a gap that a trader needs to fill and solely depends on the trader's plan. The same can be seen on either bullish or bearish pattern and it involves shooting high up or dropping depending on the mass behavior.

Position Sizing

Sizing is the number of trade units invested in a venture by a trader. Many things should be put into account when deciding the perfect position sizing that can work well with your budget and mode of business. Position sizing is the size of a position that can be reflected by the amount a trader is willing to trade with. Position sizing helps in outlining the kind of risk a trader is facing and possible ways of minimizing the loss in the long run. Some traders invest in huge dollars while some (mainly those new in the business) find it hard to trade with big cash because of the market they are not familiar with ad risks losses.

Step to Having a Correct Position Size

Every business person or trader has only one purpose and it is making profits and not accruing to losses. However, in every business, there must be a feeling of taking the risk in that is the only way to test waters by joining the business. When you are investing, take all aspects of business and determine if the venture has suitable size positioning according to plans and vision of a business

Account Risk: When you are entering the business, have in mind that you are going to try something for the first time or if not for the first time, but with different market and time and, therefore, should evaluate the risk you are facing. Every business looks at the brighter side and the darker side too just to be sure that with all the challenges, one can surely make huge profits at the close of business. What amount do you risk in your forex trading? When dealing with price action trading, it is easy to lose money as you might not interpret the mass behavior, which commonly varies according to the economy of the region where the business goes on. Any business or trade is recommended at least losing two percent in a single trade and having losses more than 2% of the initial capital is an alarming loss that needs to be checked in well.

Trade Risk: After determining the risk that an account may suffer and is pre-determined, it is also recommended for one to check the trade risk. This is where a trader trades with a limit of not losing beyond the planned mark. This means that if the business is incurring losses beyond the listed 2% of the initial capital, then it is safe to say that the business has failed.

Gap Risk: This is identifying the rate at which a trader might lose if things do not go as planned. This can be reached by making sure that the position sizing fits in well with the account risk which the investor is willing to risk per trade. With the positioning of sizes, every trader should determine how and what they want to close off their investment and the threshold that they should not surpass in taking risks.

Chapter 7: Day Trading Strategy Basics

Anyone who wishes to make money with the stock trading should have a better strategy on how to predict the trend in prices of the stock in order to maximize profits. The charts show the trends that have different patterns that a new person in the trade cannot easily interpret. The patterns in the trend have meanings that give signals to the trader on when to make a move by either buying or selling stock. These patterns are discussed below in details.

The ABCD Pattern

This is a harmonic pattern that is used to derive the other patterns of trade. This pattern is made up of three swings that are made up of the AB and CD lines, also known as the legs. The line BC is known as the correction line. The lines AB and CD are almost of the same size. The AB-CD pattern uses a downtrend that indicates that the reversal will be upward. On the other hand, the bearish pattern uses the uptrend than indicates there will be a reversal downward at some point. When using this pattern for trade, you have to know the direction of the trend and the movement of the market. There are three types of ABCD pattern; the classic ABCD pattern, the AB=CD pattern, and the ABCD extension.

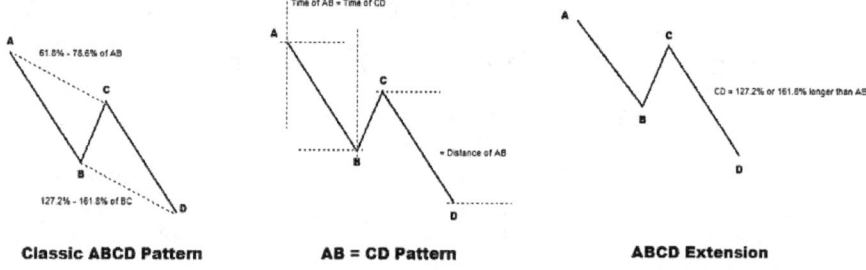

Classic ABCD Pattern   AB = CD Pattern   ABCD Extension

When using this pattern, remember that one can only enter the trade when the price has reached point D. Therefore, it is important to study the chart o at the lows and highs; you can use the zigzag indicator, which marks the swings on the chart. As you study the chart, watch the price that forms AB and BC. In a bullish trade ABCD, C should be at the lower side of A. The point A, on the other hand, should be intermediate-high after B that is at a low point. D should be a new point that is lower than B. as mentioned earlier, the entry is at point D, but when the market reaches point D, you should not be too quick to enter the trade, consider other techniques that would make sure that the reverse is up when it is a bullish trade, and down when it is a bearish trade.

Flag Momentum

In a trading market, there are times when things are good and the traders enjoy an upward trend, which gives a chart pattern that represents a bull flag pattern. It is named as such because when you look at the chart, it forms a pattern that resembles a flag on a pole. The trend in the market is an uptrend, and therefore the pattern is referred to as a bullish flag. The bull flag pattern is characterized by the following; when the stock makes a positive move with a relatively high volume, the pole is formed, when the stock consolidates on a lighter volume at the top, the flag is formed. The stock continues to move at a relatively high volume breaking through the consolidation pattern. The bull flag momentum is a trading strategy that can be used at any given time frame. When it is used to scalp the movements of price, the bull is used only on two instances of time frame: the second and the fifth minute time frames. The trading bull flags also work well when using daily charts to trade and can also be used effectively when swing trading.

It is simple to trade, but it is challenging to look for the exact bull pattern. This problem can be solved using scanners that help to look for stocks on the upward trend and wait for them to be in a consolidation position at the top. The best and free scanners that can be used to locate bull flags are Finviz and chart mill. There are tips that can be used to indicate a bull flag. When there is an increase in stock volume that is influenced by news, and when the stock prices remain high, showing a clear pattern for a pullback. At this point, you can now check out when the prices break out above the consolidation pattern or on high volumes of stock. To make a move, place a stop order at the bottom of the consolidation. At this point, the ratio of risk to reward is 2:1, and it is the best time to target. The strongest part of the pattern is the volume of the stock, and it is a good sign that there will be a major move and a successful breakout. On the trend, it is also good to look at the descending trend as it gives a sign on the next breakout. This can be seen in the trend line that is found on at the topmost of the flag.

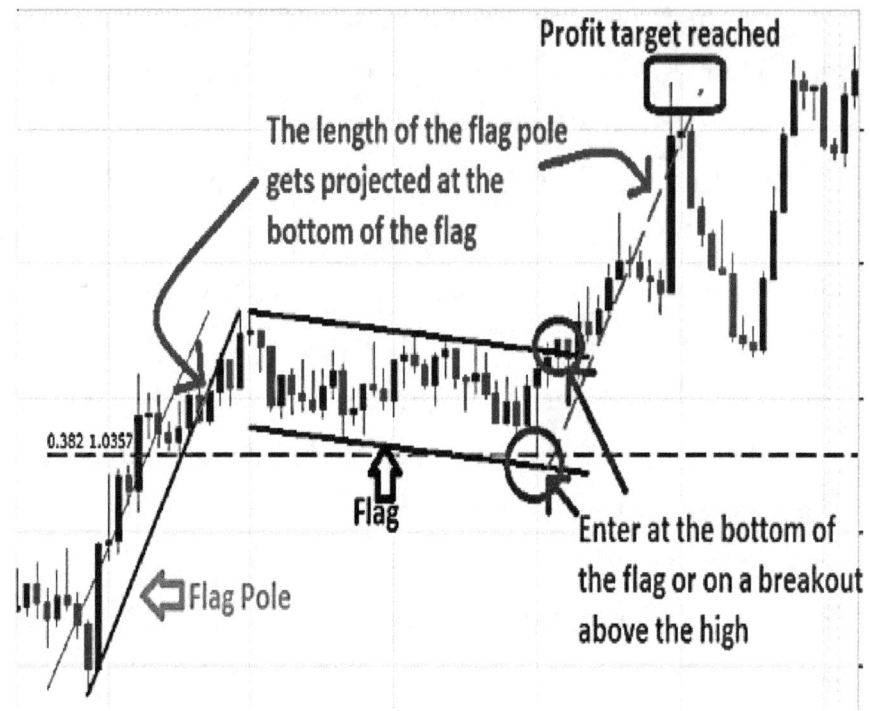

Profit target reached

The length of the flag pole gets projected at the bottom of the flag

0.382 1.0357

Flag

Flag Pole

Enter at the bottom of the flag or on a breakout above the high

When used well for trading, the bull flags are effective tools of the trade; however, things can go wrong, and therefore one must be ready with an exit strategy. There are two strategies, one is placing a stop order at a point below the consolidation area, and the second method is using a moving average that is monitored for within 20 days. Within the 20 days, if the price of the stock is below the moving average, then it is time to close out the position and try out other trading routes.

Reversal Trading

Reversal trading, also known as a trend reversal pattern, is a trading strategy that indicates the end of a trend and the start of a new one. This pattern is formed when the price level of stock in the current trend has reached a maximum. This pattern provides information on the possible change of trend and possible value of price movement. A pattern that is formed in the upwards trend signals that there would be a reversal in the trend, and the prices will go down soon. Conversely, a downward trend will indicate that there will be a movement of the prices and it will be upwards. For you to recognize this pattern, you have to know where specific patterns form in the current trend. There are distribution patterns that occur at the top of the market; at this point, traders sell more than they buy. The patterns that occur at the bottom of the markets are referred to as accumulation patterns, and at this point, traders buy more than they sell.

Reversal trends are formed at all time frames, and it is because the bank traders have either place trades are taking profits off the trades. The trend can be detected when there are multiple up and down formations that are fully formed; they should be at least two upswings and two downswings indicating a bearish pattern. The swing highs of lows on the trend line depend on which reversal pattern is formed.

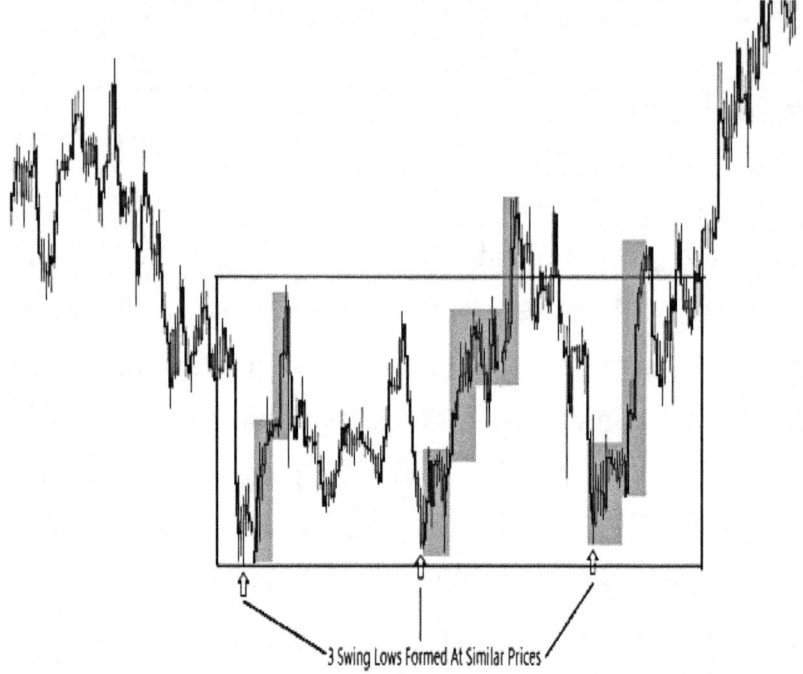

3 Swing Lows Formed At Similar Prices

The highs or lows form at a similar price because the bank traders want to appear as if they are causing a reversal in the market, by getting all their trades places at the same time. In the real sense that is not the case because they appear at different points of the trend. Therefore, as a trader, you should wait for a clear and steady trend upward for you to sell in the case of a bullish trade and a steady trend downward for the case of a bearish trade for you to buy.

There are different types of reversal patterns. The double top reversal pattern is a pattern that has two tops on the chart. It looks like "M." The double top has its reverse type known as the double bottom pattern that resembles "W." The double bottom has two bottoms located either on the same support or at different supports.

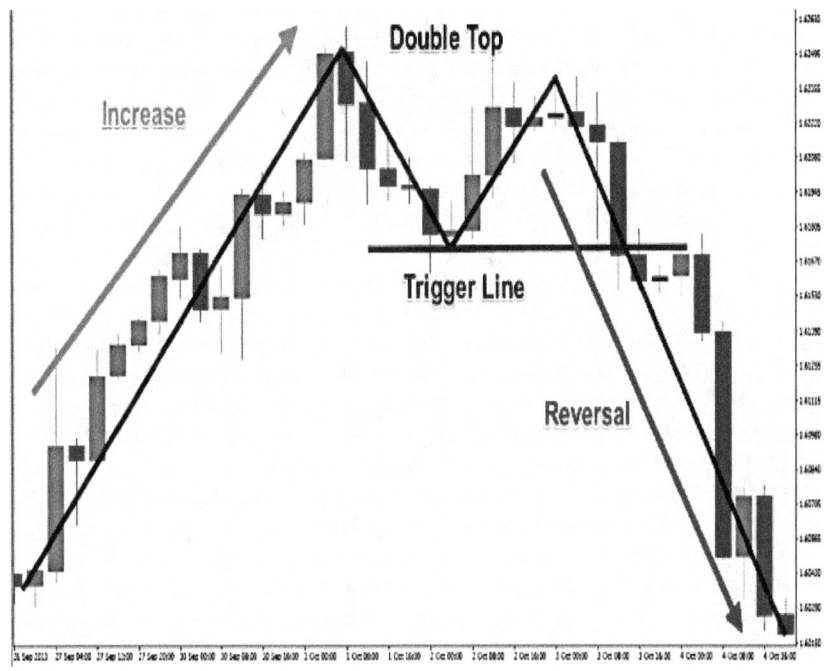

Another reversal pattern is the head and shoulders; this pattern resembled two shoulders and ahead. The two shoulders are tops that are slightly below the other top that is known as the head. The head and shoulders can also be represented in a descending pattern whereby the tops become bottoms.

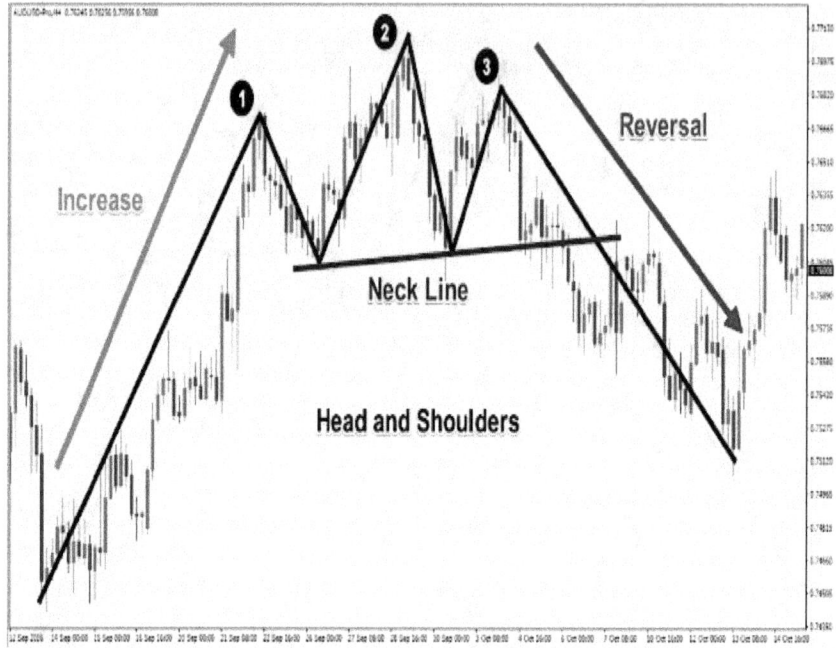

Moving Average Trend Trading

This strategy of trading is common among traders and it uses technical indicators. A moving average helps to know which way the price is moving, if the moving average is inclined upwards, then the price is moving up, and if it is inclined downwards, then the price is going downwards. Moving average can also help to show resistance or support of the trend, but this depends on the amount of time of the moving average. Support is shown when the trend of the price is downward, and at this point, the selling pressure reduces and buyers start to step in the market. Resistance is shown when the trend in the price of the stock is upward. At this point, buying of stock reduces and sellers step in. it should be noted that the prices of trade stock do not always follow the moving average, but it is good to know that when the stock price is above the moving average of the trend, then the price trend is upward. Conversely, if the price is below the moving average, then the trend of the price of the stock is downwards.

Moving average is a powerful tool of the trade as it is easy to calculate, which makes it popular among traders. This tool of trade enables the trader to understand the current trend and identify any signs of a reversal. It also helps the trader to determine entry into the trade or an exit, depending on whether it offers support or resistance.

There are different types of moving averages. The simple moving average, which sums up five recent closing prices and calculates the average price, another one is the exponential moving average, whose calculation is a bit complex because it applies more weighting to the data that is most recent. When the simple moving average and the exponential moving averages are compared, the exponential moving average is affected more by the changes in prices that the simple moving average.

VWAP Trading

VWAP is the volume-weighted average price. It is a trading strategy that is simple and highly effective when you are trading in a short time frame. For it to work for you, you must use different strategies, and the most common strategy is the waiting for a VWAP cross above and enter long. A VWAP that is across above gives signals to the traders that buyers would be entering the market, and there would be an upward movement of price. The bearish traders might short stock giving it a VWAP cross below, thus signaling the buyers to leave the market and take profits. VWAP can also be used as a resistance or support level for determining the risk of trade; when the stock trades above the VWAP, the VWAP is used as the support level, and when the trading is below the VWAP, the VWAP is used as a resistance level. In both cases, the trader is guided by the VWAP to know when to buy and when to sell.

When doing trading transactions, trading costs are determined by comparing the price of the transaction, against a reference or a benchmark, and the most common benchmark is the VWAP. The daily VWAP benchmark encourages traders to avoid risks of trading on extreme prices of the day by spreading their trades over time. This trading strategy favors those people who use market orders to trade rather than limit orders. This is because an opportunity cost arises from delays and passive trading.

Support or Resistance Trading

As traders buy and sell their stock, there are changes in the price of the stock being exchanged, and this depends on the supply and demand of a particular stock. As trade continues, there are instances where there is support or resistance in the market. Support is when the price of the stock tends to stabilize or stop falling, while resistance is when the price of the stock tends to stabilize at a point and stop to rise. These two occurrences can be used in trading; however, one must understand the trend of the trade first. Support is a level of price of the stock where the demand of the stock strong and thus prevents downward movement of the price. As the price of the stock gets near the support, the prices lower and the buyers consider it easier to buy. This reduces the number of sellers because they do not have a good deal for their stock. In this case, because the demand for the stock surpasses the supply, the price of the stock is prevented from falling below the support.

Resistance presents a case in the market that the supply is strong to control the rise of the price of the stock. In this case, as the stock price gets close to the resistance level, the price of the stock increases, making them expensive. This makes the buyers to shy away, and supply overcomes demand and therefore controls the rise in the price of the stock. There are four strategies that can be used to trade using support and resistance. The first one is using range trading, which takes place in the region between the resistance and support. In this region, buyers are trying to buy and the sellers are trying to sell. To apply this strategy, traders need to establish support and resistance on the trading chart.

The price does not always remain within the boundaries of support and resistance, and this can be risky to the traders. Therefore, to minimize losses, it is always good to set stops that are below the support when the price bounce is long and above the resistance when the bounce is short.

Another strategy is the breakout strategy. When the trade is within the region of uncertainty, there is a possibility that it will move from this region and start to trend. The point at which it starts trending is the breakout point, and all traders are always waiting for this point to maximize the change in trend. This strategy can make a good deal, but sometimes it can cause huge losses due to false breakout. It is, therefore, good to wait before committing to any trade. Trend line strategy is by drawing a line connecting many highs in the downward trend and lows in the upward trend; the trader operates along the line when wants to buy or sell.

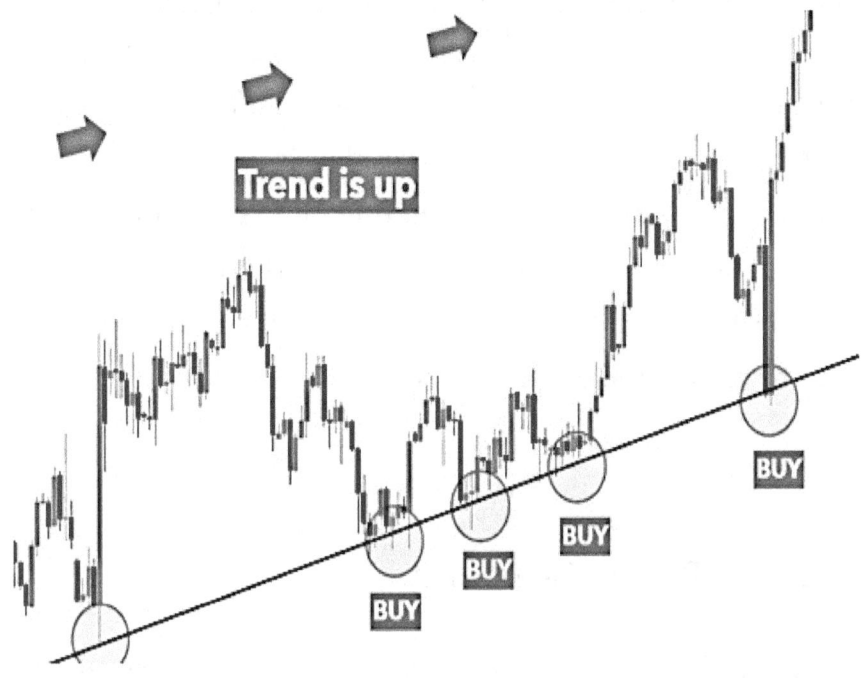

Red-to-Green Trading

Every day, stocks are traded, and each day has its own opening and closing price of a certain stock. When the price of the stock for the day is lower than the closing price of the previous day, the trade is considered red. Conversely, when it is trading at a price that is higher than the closing price, the trade is considered green. The two cases represent an opportunity of trading, depending on whether it is bullish or bearish. When the trade is bullish, the trade should make a move to trade when the trading price of the stock is higher than the previous day's closing price. However, when the trade is bearish, the trade should only make a move when the trading price of the stock is lower than the closing price of the previous day. These changes in price indicate an important shift in the trading chart, and it can easily be used to plan for trades and make profits. This strategy is best when used at the opening time of the trading day when the market is still dynamic. For those who do significant trades during the day, this strategy is good as it provides intraday trading setups.

Opening Range Breakouts

The opening time of trading is a good time to make money from your trades if you have a good plan. At this time, the market is dynamic and more active. The opening range breakdown uses reversals of the opening hour to make profits or buy at lower prices. After the market opens, it experiences highs and lows for a given period; this is the time to determine how high the stock will be during the day as well as how low in order to know the range of trading. Traders use this period to predict the price action during the day set their entry point into the market. A trader that starts to monitor the market from the time of opening is likely to notice an opportunity and maximize it. This strategy is good for full-time traders.

Before trading, one should first measure the opening range in terms of its size, and to do that you look at two candles, the last candle from yesterday's trading and the first candle that was created after the opening of the market. Calculate the difference between the last price yesterday and the first price at the opening of the market to determine the size of the opening range. In this strategy, the most important aspect is the breakout; this is because it determines how far the price will move from the opening price.

Therefore, the opening range trade strategy uses the breakout range as the entry point and those who wish to enter trade should be keen enough to choose the correct point of entry.

During the early time of market opening, the breakout range is determined by the gap and the high or low breakthrough. When using this strategy, it is you need to direct your trade towards the breakout. However, as the day progresses, the breakouts should be seen as a caution. The stop-loss order is important when using breakouts to trade in the morning, and when making estimates on how far you need to go, use the stop-loss order as the mid-point of the gap.

All the patterns discussed are useful in trading stock; it is important to understand them and know when to apply them to maximize profits. However, if you feel difficulties understanding how some of the work, it is good to master few patterns that are easy for you and trade your way to greatness in the world of FOREX and stock trading.

Chapter 8: Advanced Day Trading Strategies

When you are looking forward to capitalizing on the small, frequent price movements, day trading strategies are the best for you. Any effective strategy that you will choose must be consistent and must rely on in-depth technical analysis that utilizes charts, market patterns and price indicators predicting future price movements.

In this chapter, we will have a thorough breakdown of advanced day trading strategies. We assume that you already have good skills in money management, time management, you are educated and up to date with market events, news and economic policies, you have proper timing skills and you are consistent. It is your responsibility to choose the most appropriate strategy that best fits your requirements. The following elements will help you make the right decision: Liquidity where you are required to assess the strategy and determine if it will enable you to swiftly enter or exit a trade; volatility which will involve choosing a strategy that will tell you the potential profit range you are likely to earn. Volatility will determine the loss or profit you will make; and volume which is the measurement that will tell you the number of times a stock/asset has been traded within some given time duration. As a trader, it is good that you know the average daily trading volume. Let's have a look at the following advanced day trading strategies.

Fallen Angel

A Fallen Angel is a strategy that involves a bond that has been reduced to junk bond status from an investment-grade rating as a result of the issuer's weakening financial conditions. In terms of stock, a fallen angel refers to a stock that has always been high and now has fallen considerably. Fallen angel bonds can be a sovereign, corporate or municipal debt that a rating service has downgraded. The main reason for such downgrades could be attributed to revenue decline that generally jeopardizes the capabilities of issuers to servicing debt. The potential for downgrade often experiences a dramatic increase when expanding debts are combined with expanding debt levels. The securities of fallen angels are at times so attractive particularly to contrarian investors who seek to capitalize on the potential. This enables the issuer to recover from the temporary setback.

The downgrade process in these circumstances usually begins by placing the debt on negative credit watch. Depending on the fund-specific covenants, the portfolio managers can be required to sell their positions. The goal of this downgrading to junk status is to drive more selling pressure specifically from restricted funds to hold investment-grade debt. This, therefore, means that if the issuer can recover from the conditions that caused the downgrade, fallen angel bonds can present you very good value with a high yield.

Example

Due to the ever-falling oil prices over several quarters, an oil company has reported sustained losses. The company, therefore, can decide to downgrade its investment-grade bonds to junk status as a result of the increasing risk of default. This will result to a decline in the prices of the company's bonds and as well increase yields thus this will make the contrarian investors to be attracted to the debt as they only see the low oil prices as a temporary condition. However, there are conditions where you are likely to go at a loss especially when the fallen angel bond issuers do not recover. For example, is there is an introduction of superior products by a rival company, the issuers may fail to recover.

ABCD Pattern / Reverse ABCD Pattern

The ABCD pattern is a pattern that shows perfect harmony between price and time. ABCD pattern usually reflects the common and rhythmic style on the market movements. The geometric price/time pattern consists of three consecutive price trends with a leading indicator that can guide a trader to determine when and where to enter and exit a trade. As a trader, ABCD Pattern can be very important in identifying the available trading opportunities in any market (be it futures, forex or stock) on any timeframe (be its position, intraday or swing), and in any market condition (be it range-bound, bullish or bearish markets). Before placing a trade, ABCD Pattern can help you determine the reward and the risks of trade.

How Can You Find an ABCD Pattern?

There is both a bullish and bearish version in each ABCD pattern. The bullish pattern will help you identify the higher probability opportunities to go long or to buy. Bearish patterns will help you to identify signal opportunities to sell or to sell. On a price chart, each of the turning points in the pattern represents a significant high or a significant low. The points (A, B, C, and D) define three consecutive price trends or swings making up the AB, BC and CD pattern legs.

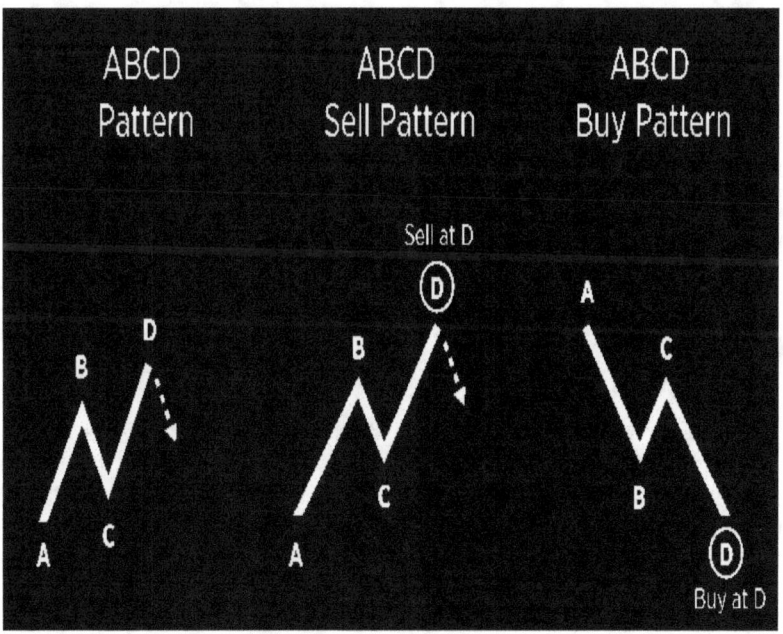

Fig. 1: A representation of the ABCD Pattern

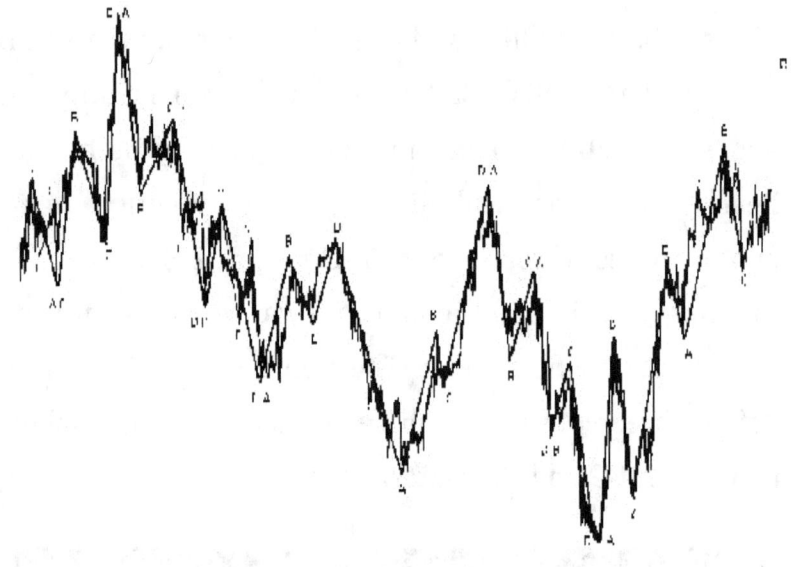

Fig. 2: ABCD pattern on a trading chart

Because trading is not an exact science, we incorporate some key Fibonacci ratio relationships which will enable us to identify proportions between AB and CD. By doing this, we will still have an approximate range completing the ABCD pattern in terms of time and price. Traders are therefore able to use these converging patterns to increase probabilities thus determining the entry and exit points inaccurate ways. On any timeframe, every pattern leg has a range of 3 to 13 candles/bars. However, there is some timeframe when the ranges can exceed 13 periods. In the cases where the ranges are over 13 bars, traders interpret it as a sign to move to a larger timeframe.

Bull Flag and Bear Flag

With technical analysis, a flag refers to a price pattern that can explode and move within a shorter timeframe to the prevailing price trend that has always been observed in longer time frames on a price chart. With the flag patterns, a trader can identify the possible prevailing a previous trend that is continuing from a given point where the price has drifted against the same trend. Therefore, in the case that the trend resumes, by noticing the flag pattern, there will be a rapid price increase and this makes the timing of a trade advantageous. Flags are areas of tight consolidation in price actions and they show a counter-trend sharp directional movement in price. This pattern has 5 to 20 price bars.

Bullish Flag Formation

These are formation patterns observed in stocks that have a strong uptrend. Bull flags got their names from the fact that the pattern closely resembles a flag on a pole. A vertical rise in-stock results to a pole and a period of consolidation results to a flag. The flag is usually angled down away from the trend that is prevailing but also can be a horizontal rectangle. The bullish flag pattern starts with a strong price spike that is almost vertical. The prices then peaks and forms an orderly pullback where the lows and the highs become almost parallel to each other making them to almost form a tilted rectangle.

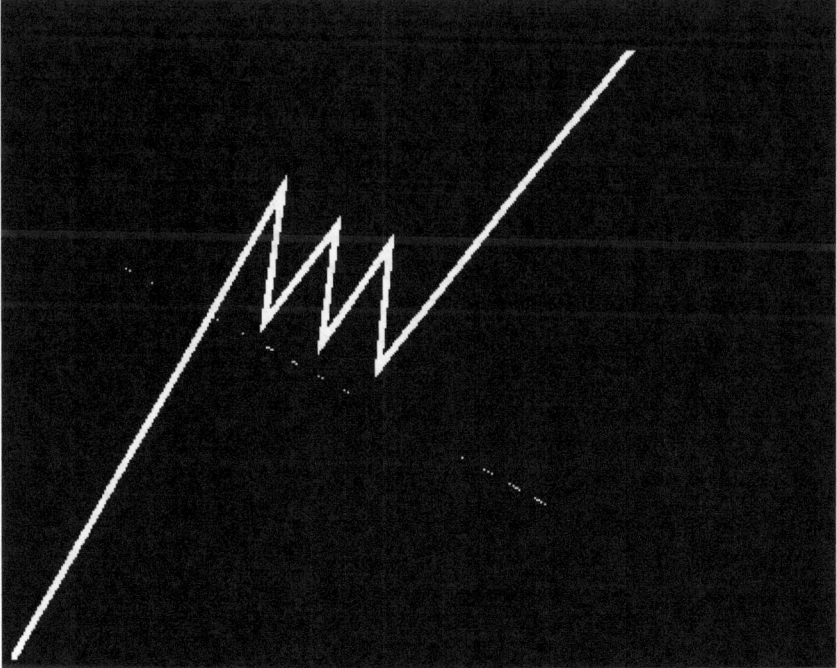

Fig 3: Bullish Flag Formation

The parallel diagonal nature is reflected by the plotted trendlines (both lower and upper trendlines). The breaking of the upper resistance trend line forms the first breakout. Another uptrend move and a breakout are formed when there is an explosion of the prices causing prices to surge back towards the high of the formation.

Bearish Flag

Comparing this flag to the bullish flag, this flag is an upside-down version of the bull flag. The bearish flag is an inverted version of the bull flag. In this case, an almost vertical panic price drop is formed by the flagpole because the sellers make the bulls to get blindsided and, as a result, there is a bounce having a parallel lower and upper trendlines, forming the flag. The panic sellers are triggered when the lower trendlines break. This flag is similar to the bull flag in that the severity of the drop on the flagpole will determine how the strength the bear flag can be.

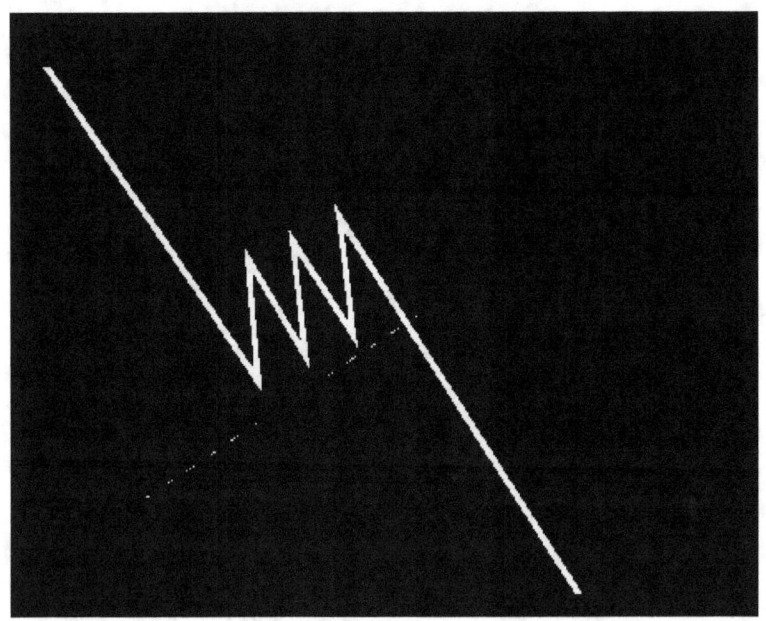

Fig. 4: The Bearish flag

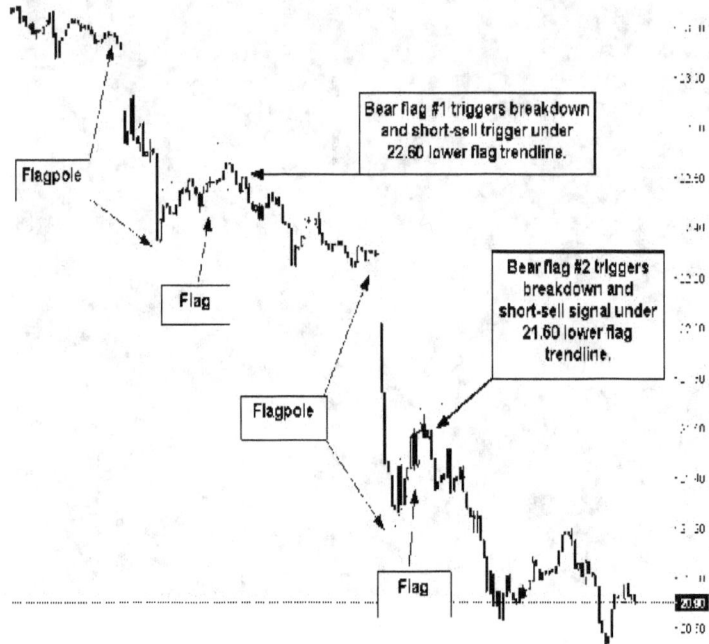

Fig. 5: The triggers in a bearish flag pattern

Planning a Trade Using Flag Patterns

As a trader, when you observe flat patterns, you need to be patient and wait for the flag to form and only then can you plot the lower and upper trendlines. The trendlines will help you know the entry and exit spots. As a trader, we advise that you use a momentum indicator like the stochastic crossover as this will effectively help you to determine and time your entries. Your stochastic crossovers should be the 80/20 band, which helps you to properly time entries and exits.

The Two Entry Spots

When you are in the trend continuation break, on any flag formation you will have, there are two entry spots. The flag break will provide you with the first entry spot and then the break on the high of the flagpole give you the second spot. Traders should capitalize on the first entry as this usually have an initial move back to the high of the flagpole, particularly before the stock breaks out or rejects.

The Trader Stop Loss Spots

There are two measured stop-loss levels in a flag pattern if the stock fails to hold its momentum. Under the upper trendlines, we can get the initial stop-loss and we can also get the precautionary trail stop on the lower trendline on downtrends. However, if you wish to avoid the wiggles, you may give it more time by placing your stop at or under the lower trendline on downtrends and the lower trendline on uptrends. We advise that you use the second trendline stop-loss as this is effective in avoiding the wiggles that trigger premature stops. The only disadvantage with this approach is that it may be costly, therefore, it is appropriate that you use lighter shares to lower your trade risks.

Target Price Levels

You can derive your targets from many indicators once you enter a flag pattern. In most cases, in the flag pattern, the high or low of the flagpole will be your initial target. You, therefore, should use fib price levels in case the price peak of the flagpole is exceeded. Fib price level targets can be obtained by plotting the high to low price levels on the flagpole. Fib price level targets can also be obtained by plotting the low to high price levels on the flagpole. Doing this will enable you to get the fib retracement and extension levels.

One Stock In-Play

Individual investors usually have a significant competitive advantage. However, only very few of these investors benefit from trade. The market has thousands of equities that investors can choose from. As a day trader, you can pick virtually any type of stock you want. Therefore, as a day trader, the first thing that you must figure out is what you should trade. We prefer that in a week, trade only one stock. It is very important that your end every week in cash. This helps you to refresh your mind and allow you to approach the following week with clear objectives and without burdens. In other words, you will also be able to enjoy your weekend. In the end, you will live a happy life. When trading with one stock in play, it is easy to trade in the market waves. For instance, you will be able to effectively focus on taking long positions, especially during an uptrend. During a downtrend, you will also be able to focus on taking short positions. Furthermore, you will be able to trade safely by being patient and pulling back things are not getting well.

Other Trading Strategies

Ichimoku Kinko Hyo

This strategy is also known as the Ichimoku Cloud. This trade strategy is a good standalone indicator that plots on the chart on top of price action. It has five lines. The first two lines form the Senkou Span, which is known as the cloud. The remaining lines are the blue Kijun Sen lines. Ichimoku Kinko Hyo is a strategy suitable for every trading asset since it has rules that are related to almost all market trends.

Strategy Rules: A trade is opened whenever the price goes out of the cloud because this will indicate that there is a potential trend that interrupts the ordinary activity of the flat price. A trader will hold the trade until the blue Kijun Sen line is interrupted by changes in price or until the day trading ends.

Stop-Loss Rules: Because a trader expected some given trend, the Kijun Sen should as well follow the price. Use a trailing stop-loss order when the closing moment moves as this will follow the price activity. Place the trailing stop-loss order on relative distance, making it be on the other side of Kijun Sen. With this, whenever the price breaks the Kijun Sen, you can always close a trade

Example

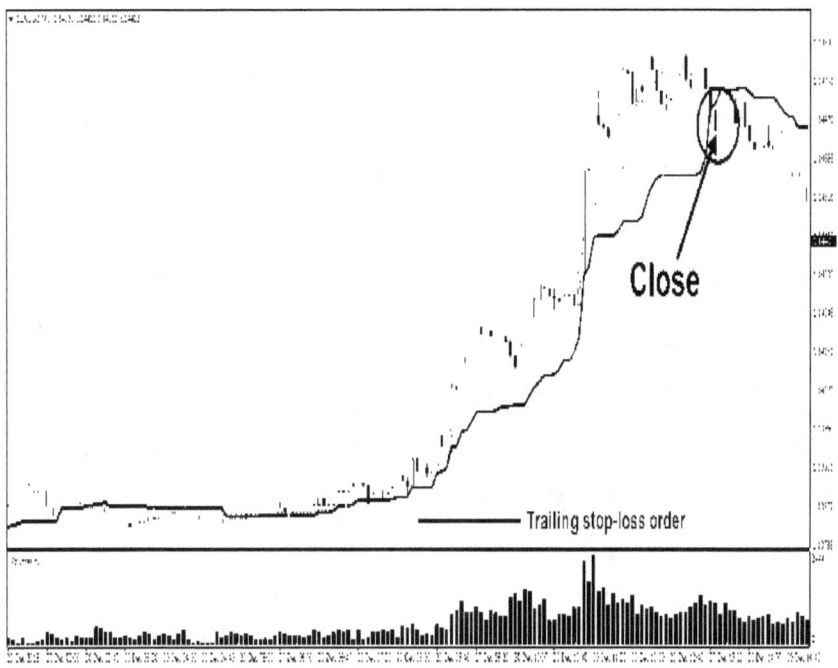

Fig. 6: A five-hour chart for EUR/USD

The chart above is a five-hour chart showing the EUR/USD currency pair for 20/12/2018. The price activity shown in the image is bullish. As the chart starts, we can see the price is inside the cloud (the Senkous Span). The green circle in the image indicates the moment when the bullish direction where the price breaks the cloud. After a few seconds, the volume indicator shows an increase in trading activity giving a trader a good reason to buy the EUR/USD pair.

The trailing stop-loss order can be put below the price action (like use 18 pips' distance). With this approach, the stop-loss crawls up and increases the price action; thus, the price will increase afterward. This trade then continues for almost 3 hours. The closing signal then comes when the price begins to break the blue Kijun Sen line. This is an indication that the bearish trend is likely to get over. Therefore, this potential trade resulted in 66 pips, which is equivalent to 0.58%. The stop-loss order risk was 0.16%, and the overall win-loss ratio from the trade is 3.63.1. This means that with a risking of 1, a trader could get a profit of 3.63.

Develop Trading Skills

To become a trader, you are required to not only know about just finance or business but also in hard science or mathematics. You must be an individual who can do deep research and analysis that can mirror the economic factors from a broader perspective as well as the day-to-day chart patterns impacting on different financial markets. As a trader, it is crucial that you need to sharpen your ability to concentrate and focus, especially in a fast-moving environment containing different people with different goals and ideas. You must also be able to practice self-control and regulate your emotions even when in situations upsetting you. Lastly, you should always be able to keep an accurate record of your trades to check on your account and to provide you with a learning opportunity that will help you become a better trader.

Chapter 9: Step-By-Step to a Successful Trade

Build A Trade Plan

Set the Rules for Exit

One of the main mistakes that most traders fail to understand is that they usually concentrate over 80% of their efforts in trying to look for signals showing buy. They, however, fail to look at where and when they should exit a trade.

Most investors will not risk selling if they are down because they are usually not ready for losses. You should get over it or else you will never make it in the trading world. Don't take things personally, especially when you are making losses. It only indicates that your predictions were incorrect. Keep it in mind that professional/experienced traders often have more losing trades that the winning trades. You will still make profits if you are able to manage your investments and limit your loses. Therefore, before entering a trade, clearly know yours exists. For every trade you do, ensure that you have at least two exit points. The first exit point is the stop-loss which will tell you to exit in the event that you are trading negatively. You should ensure that you have a written exit spot and not memorizing them. Second, ensure that you have a profit target for each trade you perform. However, don't risk more than the percentage that you have set in your portfolio. Here are exit strategies you can choose;

Exit Strategy: Traditional Stop/Limit

The most effective way to keep your emotions in check is by setting targets or limits and stops the moment a trade is entered into. You can use the DailyFX to research into the over 40 million traders. You will realize that most of the successful traders set their risk to reward ratio to at least 1:1. Before entering into a market, you have to analyze the amount of risk you are willing to assume and then set a stop at this level, while at the same time, place your target at least many pips away. This means that if your predictions were wrong, your trade would be closed automatically, and this will be at an acceptable risk level. If your prediction is correct, the trade will be closed automatically after having your target. In either way, you will still have an exit.

Exit Strategy: Moving Average Trailing Stops

This exit strategy is also referred to as a moving average. This strategy is effective in filtering the direction a currency pair has trended. The main idea behind this strategy is that traders are usually busy looking for buying opportunities, particularly when the prices are above a moving average. Traders will also be busy looking for selling opportunities, especially when the prices are moving below the average. Therefore, this strategy also considers the fact that a moving average can also be a trailing stop. This means that if a moving average cross over price, the trend is considered to be shifting. When you are a trend trader, you would consider closing out the position the moment a shift has occurred. It is preferred that you set your stop loss based on a moving average, as this is very effective.

Fig.1: Setting a trade exit using a moving average trailing stops

Exit Strategy: Volatility Bases Approach Using ATR

This technique involves the use of the Average True Range (ATR), which is designed to determine market volatility. It calculates the average range of the last 14 candles found between the high and low and thereby tells a trader the erratic behavior of the market. Traders can, therefore, use this to set stops and limits for every trade they do. A greater ATR on a given pair means a wider stop. This means if a volatile pair can generally be stopped out early, and thus will have a tight stop. You can adopt ATR for any time frame; a factor that makes to be considered as a universal indicator.

Set Entry Rules

We have set the exit rules to come before the entry rules for a reason. The reason is that exits are very important compared to entries. The entry rule is basically simple. For instance, we can have an entry rule like: "Given that signal, B fires up and we have the minimum set target is suggested to be three times the stop loss, from the fact that we give that we at service, buying Y shares or contracts here is appropriated and allowed." In as much as the effectiveness of most of these systems are determined by how complicated they are, it should also be simple enough to enable you to make effective decisions quickly. In many cases, computers usually make better trade decisions than humans and this is the reason why nearly 50% of all trades occurring today are generated on computer programs.

Computers have powerful information processing capabilities and will not want to think or rely on emotions to make decisions. If a given condition is met, then they will automatically enter. They will exit when the trade hits its profit target or when the trade goes the wrong way. Each of the decisions made by a computer is based on probabilities. Otherwise, if you rely alone on your thoughts, it will difficult for you or almost impossible to make trades.

Building an effective watchlist requires three basic steps. The first step is collecting a handful of liquidity components of leadership in each of the major sectors in the market. Secondly, you will scan through stocks that meet the general technical criteria fitting your approach to the stock market. Third, do a rescan on the list nightly to be able to identify and locate setups or patterns that can generate opportunities in the session to follow while at the same time culling out the issues you don't have interest on may be due to their technical violations or secondary offerings, etc.

Building A Watchlist

The U.S stock exchanges, for example, list more than 8,000 issues. However, a fund manager or a typical trader only access just a fraction. Why? because they have failed to come up with their effective watchlists. The main reason behind this failure is because the identification of stocks that can fully support working strategies needs some skill sets, which is usually lacking in most participants. It is therefore wise that you learn this because it will mark a trading edge that is a lifetime. For you to have a well-organized watchlist, you should have a proper understanding of the modern market environment; you need to have an understanding of how different capitalization levels impact on price development. Lastly, you should also understand how different sectors are likely to react to different catalysts over time. When choosing the candidates you want to follow, be it on a daily, weekly, or monthly basis, you have to consider economic cycles, seasonality, and sentiments.

Guidelines for Building a Watchlist

The requirements of a watchlist depend on the amount of time a trader has to do trade and as well follow the financial markets. For instance, if you are a part-timer who only plays a few positions each week, daily, you can have a simple culling list having 50-100 issues to track. Otherwise, if you are a professional trader, you have to spend more time on the task. You should build a primary database containing 350 - 500 stocks. You should also have a secondary list fitting your trading screens. Note that each trading screen should be able to accommodate between 20 and 75 issues, but this will depend on the space that charts, market depth, scanners, and news stickers windows will take. It is appropriate that to trade well, one screen should be devoted to stickers and each entry of these stickers should display just a maximum of three fields like the percentage change, the last price, and the net change. Try to link these stickers as this will enable you to have a quick review of price patterns, particularly during the trading day.

Execution

This refers to the completion of a sell or buys of an order for a security. Order execution occurs when the order gets filled and not when an order is placed by an investor. As an investor, when you submit the trade, the trade is sent to a broker. The broker determines the best way with which this trade can be executed. The law requires that brokers give the best execution possible to the investors. There is an established commission, referred to as the Securities and Exchange Commission, where brokers report the quality of their executions. Brokers are also required to notify customers whose orders were not routed for best execution. The growth of online brokers today has made the cost of trade execution to reduce significantly. Today, many traders offer a commission rebate to their customers for some set monthly targets for these customers. This can be very important for the short-term trader who tries to keep the execution costs low as possible.

There are high probabilities that you will be able to settle at the desired price if you have placed a market order or any other order that is relatively easy to be converted into a market order. However, this does not apply for all cases because there are orders that may be too large and will require that they be broken down to come up with several small orders and this might be very difficult to execute and get the best possible price range. To solve this, you can involve the use of risk in the system. Execution risk is the lag between order placement and settlement.

How Did I Do It?

Trading is a business and for you to succeed in trading, you have to treat it just the same way you would have treated any other business. As a trader, all does not stop with having knowledge on where the market has the potential to rise or fall or when to pause or reverse but rather a trader must be able to precisely determine what exact market event is going to take place and act accordingly. While trading, you have a well-written plan that is subjected to re-evaluation after the closing of a market. Your plan must be able to change with the changing market conditions. So be an individual who can adjust and improve your trading skills. Just like we have discussed in the previous sections, your plan as a trader should take into account your personal trading goals and styles. Never use another person's trading plan as this will not reflect your characteristics. A successful trade must begin by building a perfect master plant. A good trading plan will include the following;

Skill Assessment

Begin by first assessing your skills so you know whether you are ready to trade or not. Try to test your trading system by doing trading on paper and determine if you are confident that it will work. Check if you can follow your signals without any hesitation. You must have a clear mentality that trading in stock markets is like being on a battlefield that involves giving away or taking. Professional traders are always well prepared and they are ready to take profits and earn interests from those who do not have a plan and mostly give away their money as a result of their costly mistakes.

Be Mentally Prepared

Assess yourself and check how you feel, are you able to get good sleep at night? Are you feeling pressured by the challenge ahead? It is usually advised that when you are not psychologically, physically and emotionally prepared for the battle in the markets, just keep off because you are at high risk of losing your investments. This mostly happens when you get angry and act out of emotions. In many situations, traders have a market mantra that gets them ready before a day begins. It is appropriate that you create the market mantra that will always put you in a safer trading zone. Ensure that your stock trading areas are free from interruptions and distractions because, in any business, distractions are always costly.

Set Your Risk Levels

Ask yourself the risk you can handle in any trade you make. However, this is determined by your risk tolerance and trading style. On any given trading day, your portfolio should have a risk tolerance ranging between 1% - 5%. This means that on any trading day, if you happen to lose an amount that is in that range, you will get out of the trade. It is always better to fight another day.

Set Goals

An effective trader sets realistic profit targets before entering any trade. You have to assess the minimum risk/reward ratios you can accept. As observed, most pro traders will always not accept to take a trade unless the potential profit that the trade will yield is at least twice or thrice the risk. A good scenario is a case where you have a dollar loss per share in your stop-loss; therefore, your goal will be making a $3 profit. Be precise; ensure that you set your weekly, monthly and at large your annual profit goal either in as a percentage or in dollars of your trade portfolio. Regularly re-assess these goals.

Do Your At-Home Research

A trader is always informed and up to date person. Before the market opens, always ensure that you have gone through news and other sources to read what are the current trends in the world. Check whether the overseas stock and forex markets are down or up. Check whether index futures like the S&P 500 to know if they are down or up in the pre-market. The index features will provide you with the best ways to gauge the mood of the market before the opening of the market. Also, check through to know the earnings or economic data that are due. It is appropriate that you create a list that will guide you in deciding whether you would like to trade ahead of an important report or not. We prefer that you avoid taking unnecessary risks and wait for the release of the report. Pro traders don't gamble but rather they trade based on probabilities.

Trade Preparation

Always label the minor and major resistance and support levels regardless of the trading program or system you are using. Ensure that your plan also contains signals for entering and exiting a trade. Your signals should be easily detected (clear visual signal) or detected (clear auditory signal).

Always Keep Excellent Records

Professional traders keep clear records. They are interested in knowing why they won or lost a trade so that they will not make the same mistakes they made when they lost. Always ensure that you write down details like your entry and exit, goals, targets, time, market open and close, resistance and support levels and daily opening range. Always keep a record of comments on why you made a particular trade and the potential lessons you learned. Keeping trading records will help you to analyze your profits and losses for a given system; you will also be able to determine the amounts you lost per trade when you used a particular trade system. You will learn the average time you took per trade with will enable you to calculate the trade efficiency.

Chapter 10: Next Step for the Beginner Traders

Trading is very significant for merchants who want to improve their living standards. Therefore, their most considerable achievements are profits and returns. Trading is a practice that is usually accompanied by uncertainties. This aspect means the market condition of today may not be the same as the market condition of tomorrow. For that reason, there should be investors and speculators. These types of people are very different, but one thing in common is that they try to analyze the trend market to obtain good returns.

Day trading in this aspect involves buying and selling of shares, securities, futures, binaries, or the currencies to get returns. Higher returns are generated when the trading hits a positive trend. Therefore, if you have invested a lot in that area, you will fetch a proportionate pay. However, there are situations of recessions where there you can easily make losses. Such scenarios require you to apply wise business skills that are profitable. You must be a good speculator who can predict the next movement of the indicator and the point you will realize good returns. Therefore, that involves coming up with a proper trading exploration, including determining the trend analysis.

In Day trading, investors always like to risk their odds before buying and selling a stock or security closes. Brokers participate in busy transactions which are determined by the activities that constituted the number of trades they made. Forex or currencies are items that are usually traded, the strength of a currency traded with the weaker one is likely to be profitable. The charts used in day trading includes different indicators like the Moving Average Convergence and Divergence (MACD). These elements constitute the measuring of two exponential moving averages. Trade is beneficial where the scales diverge or are further away from each other. That shows that you are likely to get good returns.

There is also the Bollinger Band Indicator that measures the standard deviation of the markets of those currencies or stocks. They determine the period where that market is volatile. At a higher rate volatile market, the bands widen away from each other; however, at a lower explosive level, the indicators move close to each other.

The Relative Strength Index is very crucial when ascertaining the magnitude of the stocks overbought and the shares overbought. You may wonder what these two aspects mean; the first means that the market dealings are exceedingly bought and the other is that they are exceedingly sold. You will identify the overbought point by the higher peak of the scale and the oversold by the lower level of that indicator.

Sometimes there must be an evaluation of the point of the current rice concerning price over a given range. The methods are relevant to that investor who wants to leave the market with a sizeable profit by comparing the closing value of the stock.

Those are just a few of those indicators because they are too many. Knowledge in reading them helps one to obtain skills in predicting the next behavior of the stock or the currency you are going to trade next. To trade in such markets, you must have the necessary qualities that skilled brokers have. Remember that these people are knowledgeable in this area. Therefore, you should consider outsourcing their services. However, you can also participate in trading for yourself, which is useful in maximizing your returns and reducing the need to find a broker. The following are some of the successful tactics.

The Seven Essentials for Day-Trading for A Beginner

The first step to identify what to trade in terms of whether the securities, the stocks, or forexes. Knowing what to buy forms the action plan of what you are going to do. Otherwise, why would you even attempt the exercise if you do not identify what you should trade? It is good to have a list of all the commodities you are going to market.

The other idea that should come to your mind is when to make a purchase or sale. This signal is sufficient as it will alarm you on the best point to initiate the business. Whatever you do, make sure that point promises of good returns and not a failure. Always review the entry rule to avoid getting yourself on the loose end. For example, you use indicators like the moving average crossover. Because it has lines that are green and red, when the red and green paths cross over on each other, that should be identification in entering that to buy in that market. One ought to focus even on the long-term returns because you can realize how a promising entry idea can penetrate the market in a period to come soon.

Think of how you should make the trade. This aspect should come after brainstorming how what and when to trade. You already have the balances on the account. Therefore, the next step is how to place the money on the point you feel satisfiable. However, do you know how to make the purchase? To recognize that you should be aware of the moving indicator, see the conversion rate of currencies. Terms like the volatility, overbought, oversold should be at your fingerprints. You should recognize the different scales or indicators and their trends and movement after learning that information is your time to make a purchase.

Learn about how much you can trade. Know your financial capability and the minimum amount of money you can stake in this area. Recognize how the capital you stake will be accumulated in case of a positive trade. If you are dealing with currencies, speculate the worth of the transactions that can be achieved if you made a trade with different currencies. Know the value of different stocks and ascertain the level of profit you can immerse. After that, decide how much to put and also expectant of a possible loss.

Establish the exit rule of this business when one is gaining. How to exit the market is vital because some individuals may make returns at a point where they are influenced to trade again, which can lead to a loss in those gains. Therefore, you have to know the spot to exit that business. Reflect the example earlier of the Dual Moving Average Crossover (DMAC), where if short term line crosses the long-term line, it produces the sell signal. Do not wait for the bell to ring, otherwise exit immediately on the market. You will realize the significant profit you will gain.

Conversely, you can also detect how to cite a losing position. Some trends with a winning margin but they significantly fall. Do not wait to make further losses at that area at a belief that it will soon pick. One has to identify the protective stops that indicate the stock is seemingly fluctuating. This stop is realized when a trader has views on the behavior of the scale after it is opened. The limit beyond that closure is what is referred to as the protective stop. Therefore, make thorough assessments of this juncture to exit any markets that portray such behavior.

Finally, ask yourself what to do if you have insufficient capital. There usually are constraints of the open trade that instable adequate financial balance. The system should address how the trader can do at the insufficiency of funds. And use of the MODUS method, in this case, is relevant because it analyses the uncommitted funds, and there is free capital that refuses to balance. Therefore, avoid the trader's system, which does not address this issue.

Elements of Day-Trading Specialists That Beginners Should Have

How best can something be if it is earning you that extra penny? It is further compelling if you are collecting this money at the comfort of your couch while glaring on your computer or the phone. If you are skilled in speculation and prediction, then this business model is the right for you. Remember that the discussion point here is about the day-trading business. One thing is that you need adequate preparation. Do not be afraid you feel you are less literate to online trading; however, gather for more information about the business. You will soon gain confidence as you prepare to make a purchase. Gather information about the indicators available and if you are dealing in currencies, learn how those currencies even fair in the real market. Ensure that you are sitting comfortably, moreover, ensure your computer is well set. Ascertain that even the internet connection is god, it would be hurting if you experience an electric breakdown amid the exciting opportunity to harvest superb returns.

Be confidence in every point you try to make a trade. That confidence is further boosted by keeping everything simple. Remember that you have adequate time to learn the movement of the prices and indicators. Do not rush even if you feel you are nearing a jackpot that may trick you in speculating all your cash. Therefore, take the time to carry this activity. Moreover, try to concentrate on a single type of trade as many types may confuse you.

Achieving your goals is the best part of this activity. In this case, your goals are the returns you aim. However, do not be over ambitious as this will ruin your chances of winning. When one is over-ambitious, it means setting they are setting unrealistic and unattainable goals. Imagine putting a small cent and expecting more significant profit margins if you want to gain more, and you have to risk more. Know that this game is all about risk-taking. Hence you should be ready to make even more significant losses.

Risk management is primarily the critical characteristic of success in this business. The roots of this trade are very bitter, but its fruits are sweet. Get that idea in your head and do not be afraid of losing. You may consistently loose, but you will eventually score a significant return. It is reported that most of the risk-takers use more than a percentage of their account. You can even riskily juggle with your money on every point the indicator moves. You will eventually study the pattern and trend, and at last, you will hit the jackpot.

Keep a record of your transactions and your daily outcomes of the investment. Even when you register losses and profits, do not forget to file them. Remember that the investment should be a hobby that you can record even in a diary. By that practice, you can analyze the dealings you had and assess where you went wrong to address the pitfalls. You can be surprised that those worksheets can help you in tracing a pattern of the trade in which you can use the skills to immerse higher profits.

Timing is always a factor in this operation. Even some indicators like the Stochastics, Relative Strength Index, or the MACD do have a time factor. It all depends on the point you identify the peak of the indicator. Always carry with you a stopwatch to ensure even that seconds are not lost. You might rely on that the profitable point that changes with seconds. Therefore, you must be fast before that second pass you. Always be on the lookout to manage time properly where it should not be disrupted.

You must make a sensible decision making. This field is where your prowess in making critical decisions is tested. Some wrongful choices you make can earn you a painful loo. If you find yourself willing to place your odds at a particular point, first consult yourself if that is the most profitable place. You must be fast in decision making, and you should be assertive in the resolution you make. Always make intuitive decisions because the conscience can help one to sensitize a potentially profitable point.

Trial and error is another secret to success. However lucky you are, it is sometimes hard to make successful moves or the time. You must fail in one of them if not all. Do not fear to lose all the money in the account, and even you can use the demo and try that trial and error technique. This approach will consequently sharpen your skills in trading.

Conclusion

Thank you for making it through to the end of *Day Trading Strategies*, let's hope it was informative and able to provide you with all of the tools and information you need to manage your journey in the market trade.

Day trading is described as the process of speculation of risks and either buying or selling of financial instruments on the same day of trading. The financial instruments are bought at a lower price and later sold at a higher price. People who participate in this form of trade are mostly referred to as speculators. Day trading is the different form of trading known as swing trading. Swing trading involves selling of financial instruments and latter buying them at a lower price. It is a form of trade that has several people have invested their time and capital in. The potential for making profits is very high. However, it is also accompanied by the high potential of making huge percentages of loss. People who are terms as high-risk takers have the potential to realize good amounts of profits or huge losses. It is because of the nature of the trade. The losses are experienced because of several variables that are always present in trading. The gains and individual experiences are brought to light by margin buying.

There as a big difference between swing trade and day trade. The difference hails from their definitions, it goes a mile ahead to time spent in and risks involvement in both forms of trade. Day trade has lower risk involvement, but one has to spend more of his or her time, unlike swing trade. Day traders are prone to participating in two forms of trade which are long trades or short trades. Long trade involves an individual purchasing the financial instruments and selling them after them increasing in value. On the other hand, short trade involves selling financial instruments and later purchasing them after their prices have dropped.

The trading market has undergone through several advancements. The major change was witnessed during the deregulation process. There was the creation of electronic financial markets during this period. One of the major innovations was the high-frequency trading index. It uses heavy algorithms to enable huge financial firms in stock trading to perform numerous orders in seconds. It is advantageous because it can also predict market trends.

The process of day trading has several challenges. An individual is supposed to be able to make a good decision during two important moments. The first moment is during a good streak and the other is during moments an individual has a poor run.

At this point risk management and trading, psychology comes in handy to help an individual in the trade. One is not supposed to panic or make hasty decisions during these moments. It is important for an individual to have an effective watchlist. A good watchlist built by a trader is supposed to be able to understand the modern trading markets. This is made possible when it features stocks in play, float and market capital, pre-market grippers, real-time intraday scans, and planning trade based on scanners. The success of day trading is also incumbent on effective strategies. The common strategies include ABCD patterns, bag flag momentum, reversal trading, movie average trading, and opening range breakouts.

There are also advanced strategies that can be used to ensure the success of day trading. Three of these strategies are one stock in play, bull flag, and a fallen angel. With the use of these strategies, a successful trader builds his or her trading business step by step. The common steps involve building a watchlist, having a trading plan and knowing how to execute. There are also simple steps that can be followed by beginners.

The End

www.ingramcontent.com/pod-product-compliance
Lightning Source LLC
Chambersburg PA
CBHW070340220526
45467CB00001B/197